Wellone Ecyes 2000

Happy Cooking

Conrad gallagher

one pot wonders

one pot wonders

Conrad Gallagher

with photographs by Gus Filgate

GILL & MACMILLAN

To Lauren, with all my love

Edited by Alexa Stace

Photography by Gus Filgate

Styling by Helen Trent

Designed by Mark Latter @ Vivid

Colour Reproduction by Sang Choy

Production by Lorraine Baird & Sha Huxtable

Published in Ireland in 2000 by

Gill & Macmillan Ltd

Goldenbridge, Dublin 8

with associated companies throughout the world

www.gillmacmillan.ie

ISBN 0 7171 3053 3

Thanks to Sophie without whom this book would never have been

completed.

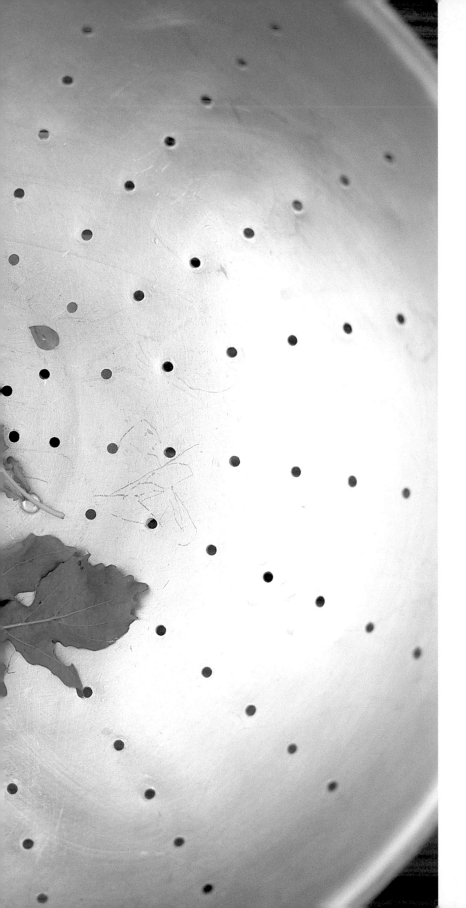

contents

introduction

The idea for this book is a simple one. The recipes are designed so that with a little thought and preparation – and sometimes even with none at all – they can be cooked using just one pan. In many cases you can even serve them in the pan.

The reasoning behind this is simple. By imposing the one-pan discipline I forced myself to simplify some of the more complicated dishes we serve in our restaurants. I feel that this makes the dishes less intimidating to people who would like to try something different, but who do not necessarily possess a huge kitchen and a massive arsenal of cookware. Plus it saves on the washing up. After all, when you are cooking at home for friends and family, no matter how much you enjoy it you should aim to spend more time eating the food than you do cooking it – or clearing up afterwards. It is an essential part of my philosophy that food can be sophisticated, yet simple; that meals can be classy, without being complicated. In our restaurants we are blessed with a large staff, lots of space and an impressive array of equipment. And even when we are under immense pressure we still have plenty of time to devote to preparation. At home you may not have any of that, but just because you are short of time, space or equipment doesn't mean that you can't produce great-tasting, good-looking food which is fun to cook and enjoyable to eat.

I've always believed that food – whether eating out in a restaurant or at home – should be an enjoyable experience. When you cook at home there's a reason why it's called entertaining – it should be! I hope that *One Pot Wonders* will help with that, and that it encourages you to experiment further in your own kitchen.

RESTAURANT

PEACOCK

ALLEY

saucepan

In my restaurants I always use copper-lined saucepans. Copper conducts heat evenly and ensures that ingredients do not get scorched at high temperature and during quick cooking. Copper pans are expensive, but they are a good investment if you do cook a lot, as they can last for years if well maintained. Otherwise stainless steel saucepans are readily available and are excellent for one-pot cooking.

In the South of France they serve this for breakfast during the asparagus festival. Slices of black truffle add a luxurious touch, and diced truffle gives the hollandaise sauce a heavenly, unforgettable aroma.

asparagus with poached egg

and truffle hollandaise

you will need

8 quail's eggs

1 tbsp wine vinegar

16 asparagus spears, blanched

2 tbsp melted butter

16 rocket leaves (optional)

8 thin slices of black truffle (optional)

Selection of chopped herbs, to garnish

1 tomato, peeled, deseeded and chopped

TRUFFLE HOLLANDAISE

1 shallot, finely diced

50ml/2fl oz white wine

1 tbsp chopped fresh thyme

4 egg yolks

250g/8oz butter, diced

2g/⅙oz black truffle, finely diced

Serves 4

First make the hollandaise. Place the shallot, white wine and thyme in a medium-sized pan. Bring to the boil and cook until reduced by half. Remove from the heat and transfer to a bowl. Rinse out the pan, fill with water and bring to the boil.

Add the egg yolks to the bowl and whisk, then place the bowl in the pan of boiling water. Remove the pan from the heat and gradually add the diced butter, whisking continuously. Each time, allow the butter to melt and the sauce to thicken before adding more. If you think the sauce is going to separate, take the bowl out of the pan and add a few teaspoons of cold water. Continue until all the butter has been added. Add the diced truffle and keep warm in a bain-marie until ready to use.

Bring the water back to the boil and preheat the grill. Add the vinegar to the pan and poach the eggs until soft, then transfer to a bowl of cold water until ready to use.

Place the asparagus under the grill and brush with the butter. Grill lightly for 1 minute on each side, then arrange on a serving dish on a bed of rocket leaves, if using. Reheat the eggs in a bowl of boiling water, then drain. Arrange the slices of truffle on top of the asparagus, and top each slice with a quail's egg. Drizzle with the hollandaise, and garnish with a selection of fresh herbs and chopped tomato.

I first sampled morels in the West of Ireland in 1985, roasted with garlic and parsley, and I can still remember the taste. Wanting that taste becomes a craving, like waiting for the truffle season, and my order is always in early, so that morels are sure to be on the menu while they are in season.

peas & morels
with fried quail's eggs

you will need

1kg/2lb fresh shelled peas

Salt and freshly ground

black pepper

3 tbsp olive oil

50g/2oz butter

6 shallots, diced

2 tsp chopped rosemary

2 tsp chopped thyme

2 cloves garlic, crushed

250g/8oz morels, stems trimmed

300ml/½ pint Chicken Stock

  (see page 153)

150ml/¼ pint double cream

100ml/3½fl oz Beef Jus (see page 157)

4 quail's eggs

Flat-leaf parsley sprigs, to garnish

Serves 4

Cook the peas in a pan of boiling salted water for 2–3 minutes. Refresh in cold water, drain, pat dry and set aside. Rinse out the pan.

Place the olive oil and 40g/1½ oz of the butter in the pan over moderate heat. Add the shallots, rosemary, thyme and garlic and sauté for 3–4 minutes. Add the peas, morels, chicken stock, cream and beef jus to the pan and cook for another 2–3 minutes.

Transfer the mixture to a large bowl and keep warm. Rinse out the pan. Melt the remaining butter in the pan and lightly fry the quail's eggs. Serve the peas and morels with the eggs on top and garnish with sprigs of parsley.

Dublin Bay prawns are the best, and the freshest. The prawn shells are first sautéed in olive oil with garlic and shallots then simmered in chicken stock, giving an added depth of flavour to the rich, creamy pasta sauce.

linguine

with dublin bay prawns

Cook the linguine in a pan of boiling salted water for 8 minutes, or until al dente. Drain, refresh in cold water and drain again. Rinse out the pan.

Heat 1 tablespoon of the olive oil in the pan until it is smoking. Add the prawns and sauté for 1 minute on each side. Remove from the pan and reserve.

Heat the remaining oil in the pan until it is smoking. Add the prawn shells, garlic and shallots and sauté for 3 minutes. Add the tomato purée and chicken stock, bring to the boil, and simmer until reduced by half. Add the cream and simmer for 5 minutes. Pour the sauce through a fine sieve and adjust the seasoning.

Return the sauce to the pan and mix in the linguine, peas, tarragon and prawns. Heat gently to warm through, tossing well. Season to taste and serve.

you will need

200g/7oz dried linguine

2 tbsp olive oil

20 Dublin Bay prawns, shelled and deveined, shells reserved

1 clove garlic, crushed

2 shallots, finely chopped

25g/1oz tomato purée

600ml/1 pint Chicken Stock (see page 153)

600ml/1 pint double cream

Salt and freshly ground black pepper

50g/2oz garden peas, blanched

15g/½oz tarragon leaves

Serves 4

garlic mash

Place the potatoes in a pan of salted water. Bring to the boil, reduce the heat and cook for 20 minutes, or until the potatoes are tender. Drain, mash and transfer to a bowl. Rinse out the pan.

Place the cream and garlic in the pan and cook gently until reduced by a quarter. Strain, add the butter and allow it to melt. Add the cream mixture to the potatoes and mix well. Reheat and season if necessary.

you will need

8-12 potatoes, peeled and cubed

Salt

200ml/7fl oz double cream

3 cloves garlic

100g/3½oz butter

Serves 4

Heavenly Italian scents and flavours combine to magnificent effect in this simple but impressive pasta recipe.

pappardelle with prosciutto,
rocket, pine nuts and parmesan

you will need

275g/9oz dried pappardelle

Salt and freshly ground black pepper

3 tbsp Basil Pesto (see page 155)

75g/3oz prosciutto, diced

50g/2oz pine nuts

100g/3½oz grated Parmesan

1 large handful rocket leaves

Serves 4

Cook the pappardelle in a large pan of boiling salted water until al dente, then drain well and return to the pan over a low heat. Add the pesto and mix into the pappardelle. Add the prosciutto, pine nuts and Parmesan and toss well.

Stir in the rocket until just wilted, adjust the seasoning and serve immediately.

Flavoured risottos are very fashionable, using everything from squid ink to fresh herbs, but this is my favourite. In the States I always loved the pumpkin season, and this risotto is the perfect dish for an autumnal flavour.

pumpkin risotto

with trompettes de mort and pancetta

you will need

25g/1oz butter

2 shallots, finely diced

1 clove garlic, crushed

1 tsp thyme

250g/8oz arborio rice

200ml/7fl oz white wine

1 litre/1¾ pints hot Vegetable Stock (see page 153)

100ml/3½ fl oz double cream

50g/2oz Parmesan, grated

75g/3oz pancetta, thinly sliced

100g/3½ oz trompettes de mort sautéed in

50g/2oz butter

4 tbsp mascarpone

1 tbsp diced red pepper, to garnish

PUMPKIN PURÉE

2 small pumpkins, peeled, deseeded and diced

2 cloves garlic, crushed

4 tbsp olive oil

3 sprigs thyme

Serves 4

For the purée, preheat the oven to 200°C/400°F/Gas mark 6. Place the pumpkin in a heavy-based, ovenproof pan with the garlic, olive oil and thyme. Roast for 30 minutes, then remove from the oven and allow to cool. Transfer to a food processor, blend until smooth, then push through a fine sieve into a bowl. Rinse out the pan.

For the risotto, melt the butter in the pan. Add the shallots, garlic and thyme, cover and sweat over a medium heat until soft. Add the rice and white wine. Cover and sweat for about 2 minutes on a medium heat, then uncover and reduce until almost dry. Gradually add the vegetable stock to the rice, stirring continuously after each addition until all the stock has been absorbed and the rice is tender.

Mix the cream and the Parmesan into the risotto, then mix in the pumpkin purée. Serve in bowls and arrange the pancetta and trompettes de mort on top. Add a spoonful of mascarpone to each serving and garnish with the diced pepper.

The secret of making perfect risotto is to use good-quality rice and a well-flavoured stock. It is important to add the hot stock gradually, stirring well after each addition until the liquid is absorbed.

gorgonzola
and red onion risotto

you will need

2 tbsp olive oil

2 large shallots, diced

1 large red onion, finely diced

100ml/3½ fl oz dry white wine

250g/8oz risotto rice, such as arborio

1 tsp thyme

1 tbsp double cream

1 tbsp Gorgonzola

1 litre/1¾ pints hot Chicken Stock (see page 153)

25g/1oz butter

Salt and freshly ground black pepper

1 tbsp grated Parmesan

Serves 4

Heat the oil in a heavy-based pan over moderate heat. Add the shallots and red onion, cover and sweat for 3–4 minutes until soft. Add the white wine and simmer until reduced by half. Bring to the boil and add the rice and thyme.

Start adding the hot stock gradually, stirring after each addition until all the liquid has been absorbed. When all the stock has been absorbed and the rice is tender, stir in the cream, Gorgonzola and butter. Season with salt and pepper and sprinkle with the grated Parmesan before serving.

Fresh spring vegetables lend their name to this delicately flavoured risotto,
a perfect vehicle for serving up the first asparagus of the season.

risotto primavera

Melt 50g/2oz of the butter with the olive oil in a heavy-based pan over moderate heat. Add the garlic and shallot and sauté for 3–4 minutes or until soft.

you will need

100g/3½oz butter

1 tbsp olive oil

1 clove garlic, crushed

1 shallot, finely diced

250g/8oz arborio or other risotto rice

1 litre/1¾ pints hot Vegetable Stock

(see page 153)

100g/3½oz baby spinach

100g/3½oz fresh peas, blanched until tender

12 asparagus spears, blanched until tender

and cut into 2.5cm/1in pieces

90ml/3fl oz white wine

Salt and freshly ground black pepper

2 tbsp double cream

25g/1oz parsley, chopped

100g/3½oz grated Parmesan

Serves 4

Add the rice, stir well and cook for 2 minutes. Start adding the stock gradually, stirring continuously after each addition until the liquid is absorbed. When most of the liquid has been absorbed and the rice is tender add the vegetables and white wine, mix well and cook for 1 minute.

Remove from the heat, season with salt and pepper and add the remaining butter, the cream, chopped parsley and Parmesan. Mix well and serve at once.

Orzo are small pasta shapes which look like grains of rice. They make an attractive presentation in this one-pot dish which would be ideal for a quick lunch or supper.

orzo with feta,

mint and plum tomatoes

Cook the orzo in boiling salted water until al dente, then drain, rinse under cold water, and drain again thoroughly.

Mix in the remaining ingredients, season well and serve garnished with mint or rocket leaves and sundried tomatoes.

you will need

250g/8oz orzo

Salt and freshly ground black pepper

50ml/2fl oz extra virgin olive oil

Juice of 2 lemons

2 tbsp finely chopped mint

200g/7oz feta cheese, diced

4 plum tomatoes, finely diced

100g/3½oz good quality stoned
   black olives

Mint or rocket leaves and sundried
   tomatoes, to garnish

Serves 4

Polenta cakes, cut into rounds with a biscuit cutter, make an attractive accompaniment to fish or poultry. They need to be well flavoured, so add a good selection of fresh chopped herbs.

polenta cake with goat's cheese
and herbs

Heat the milk, cream, butter, shallots and garlic together in a heavy-based pan. Bring to the boil, then reduce the heat to a simmer. Slowly add the polenta in a thin stream, stirring constantly with a wooden spoon. Continue to simmer on the lowest heat, stirring frequently, until the mixture is thick and comes away from the sides of the pan. The polenta will lose its corn taste after about 45 minutes.

Stir in the goat's cheese and herbs and cook for 1–2 minutes. When cooled, spread out about 1cm/½in inch thick on a flat tray and leave to set. When cold, cut out rounds using a 5cm/2in cutter. To serve, reheat in the oven, shallow-fry in olive oil or grill on both sides until golden.

you will need

500ml/16fl oz milk

150ml/¼ pint double cream

15g/½oz butter

2 shallots, finely chopped

1 garlic clove, crushed

500g/1lb polenta

100g/3½oz goat's cheese

Handful of herbs, such as basil,

chives, coriander, chervil,

finely chopped.

Serves 4

This dish is true fusion. Harissa, a hot sauce which comes from North Africa and is often served with couscous, is teamed with a spicy Indian masala sauce to give zest to these unusual medallions – of kangaroo, not beef.

kangaroo medallions

with harissa and spicy masala sauce

To make the sauce, dry-roast the shrimp paste in a large, heavy-based pan over a medium heat. Add the oils and fry the onion, garlic, ginger, galangal, chilli, turmeric and coriander roots. Add the dried prawns and spices. Stir in the tomato purée, coconut cream and palm sugar and cook on a gentle heat until the mixture starts to bubble. Add the stock, bring to the boil, then simmer for 1 hour until reduced by at least half. Skim off any excess oil and scum, remove from the heat and pass through a sieve into a jug. Add the fish sauce and season to taste. Rinse out the pan.

Mix the pepper and coriander and sprinkle over the medallions, then brush with olive oil. Heat the pan until very hot and sear the meat for about 2–3 minutes on both sides, depending on how rare you like it. Spoon some sauce around each plate, place a medallion in the centre and add a teaspoon of harissa on top of the meat. Serve with fresh vegetables.

you will need

1 tsp black peppercorns, ground

1 tsp coriander seeds, ground

4 x 150g/5oz kangaroo medallions

Olive oil

6 tsp harissa

Fresh vegetables, to serve

SPICY MASALA SAUCE

2 tsp shrimp paste

5 tbsp vegetable oil

2 tbsp sesame oil

1 onion, finely chopped

4 cloves garlic, finely chopped

1 tbsp finely chopped root ginger

2 slices galangal, finely chopped

5 red chillies, deseeded and finely chopped

2 slices of turmeric, finely chopped

4 coriander roots, crushed

1 tsp sichuan peppercorns, ground

2 tsp dried prawns, roasted and ground

1 tsp cumin seeds, ground

2 tsp coriander seeds, ground

1 tsp turmeric powder

Pinch of freshly grated nutmeg

8 fresh curry leaves

1 stick cinnamon

100ml/3½fl oz tomato purée

150ml/¼ pint coconut cream

50g/2oz palm sugar, shaved

1.25 litres/2 pints Beef Stock (see page 153)

2 tbsp fish sauce

Serves 4

The combination of parmesan and coconut is unusual, but it works very well in this simple but effective pasta dish.

fettuccine with squash,

spring onions, parmesan and coconut

Preheat the oven to 180°C/350°F/Gas mark 4. Roast the squash in the preheated oven for 15 minutes. Remove from the oven and allow to cool, then peel, deseed and cut into 1cm/½in cubes.

you will need

1 medium butternut squash

1 bunch spring onions, sliced

Salt and freshly ground black pepper

400g/13oz dried fettuccine

2 tbsp olive oil

1 x 400g/13oz can of coconut cream

25g/1oz grated coconut

25g/1oz grated Parmesan

Serves 4

Blanch the onions in a large pan of boiling water for 1 minute. Refresh under cold water and pat dry. Salt the boiling water, add the pasta and cook until al dente. Drain and set aside.

Rinse out the pan, then heat the olive oil over medium heat. Add the squash and spring onions, cover and sweat for 3–4 minutes. Add the coconut cream and simmer for 5 minutes. Stir in the grated coconut, season to taste and remove from the heat. Add the pasta, toss well to heat through and serve sprinkled with grated Parmesan.

deep pan

The wok is ideal for one-pot cooking - quick and easy, and almost impossible to get wrong! In the West woks are mostly used for stir-frying, but in Asian cooking they are also used for boiling, steaming and deep-frying. Keep your wok well oiled, to prevent it going rusty, and wipe it out with kitchen paper after use, rather than washing it.

I adore pumpkin, but butternut squash makes a lovely alternative. The cumin cream gives this soup a wonderfully smooth, nutty flavour.

butternut squash soup

with cumin cream

To make the cumin cream, pour the cream into a bowl and stir in the lemon juice. Fold in the ground cumin and season with salt and pepper.

you will need

1kg/2lb butternut squash, peeled and cut into thick chunks

900ml/½ pints Chicken Stock (see page 153)

300ml/½ pint crème fraîche

2 tbsp butter

Salt and freshly ground black peppeer

Several chives, cut into 2.5cm/1in lengths

CUMIN CREAM

500ml/17fl oz double cream

Juice of 2 lemons

50g/2oz ground cumin

Serves 4

Place the squash and the stock in a large pan over a high heat. Bring to the boil, then reduce the heat and simmer for 20 minutes. Remove from the heat and allow the mixture to cool, then purée until smooth in a blender.

Return the purée to the pan over a medium heat. Stir in the crème fraîche, cumin cream, butter, salt and pepper. Stir until heated through, adding more seasoning if necessary. Serve garnished with the chives.

This is a classic Thai dish – hot, spicy and sweet. It is very popular, but it is difficult to find it cooked properly. This is how it should be done.

thai chicken & coconut soup

with shiitake mushrooms

Heat 2 tbsp of the olive oil and the butter in a large pan over a low heat. Add the lemongrass, shallots, garlic, spring onions, thyme and rosemary, cover and sweat for 3–4 minutes. Add the peanut butter and stir until smooth.

Pour in the coconut milk, bring to the boil and simmer until reduced by half. Add the chicken stock and wine and bring back to the boil, then pour in the cream. Remove from the heat and allow to cool. Purée the soup in a food processor, then pass through a fine sieve into a bowl.

Rinse the pan, then heat the remaining olive oil over a low heat. Add the shiitake mushrooms, chillies and beansprouts. Cover and sweat for 3–4 minutes. Add the soup and chicken breast and heat through gently.

Serve sprinkled with chopped fresh coriander.

you will need

100ml/3½ fl oz olive oil

50g/2oz butter

2 stalks lemongrass, chopped

3 shallots, finely chopped

2 cloves garlic, crushed

1 bunch spring onions, finely chopped

1 tbsp thyme leaves

1 tbsp rosemary leaves

1 tsp peanut butter

250ml/8fl oz coconut milk

600ml/1 pint Chicken Stock (see page 153)

100ml/3½ fl oz white wine

100ml/3½ fl oz double cream

250g/8oz shiitake mushrooms, chopped

2 chillies, deseeded and finely diced

50g/2oz beansprouts

4 chicken breasts, skinned, poached and diced

Chopped coriander, to garnish

Serves 4

This is a peasant fish soup done in gourmet style to make it rich and creamy, with the subtle, spicy flavours of South-East Asia.

john dory soup

with coconut and curry

you will need

50ml/fl oz olive oil

75g/3oz lemongrass, chopped finely

10 shallots, sliced

3 cloves garlic, sliced

3 sprigs thyme

5 curry leaves

2.5cm/1in root ginger, peeled and grated

100g/3½oz butter

2 tbsp curry powder

3 tbsp turmeric

1.5 litres/2½ pints Chicken Stock (see page 153)

500ml/17fl oz double cream

250ml/8fl oz coconut milk

2 tbsp coconut cream

1kg/2lb John Dory fillets, skinned

Salt and freshly ground black pepper

shredded lettuce, to serve

chillies, whole and sliced, to garnish

Serves 6

Place the olive oil in a large pan over a low heat. Add the lemongrass, shallots, garlic, thyme, curry leaves and ginger, cover and sweat for 5 minutes. Stir in the butter, curry powder and turmeric. Add the chicken stock and cream, and bring to the boil. Simmer for 10 minutes then add the coconut milk and coconut cream.

Pass the soup through a fine chinois sieve, then reheat and add the fish fillets. Cover and simmer gently for 3–5 minutes or until the fish is cooked. Season to taste and serve garnished with shredded lettuce and chillies.

For those who adore shellfish this is quick, simple – and irresistible.
The sharp tang of watercress and lime is a delightful surprise.

mussels & clams

with lime and watercress

you will need

100ml/3½fl oz white wine

48 small mussels, scrubbed and rinsed, with
beards removed

24 small clams, rinsed

90ml/3fl oz olive oil

Zest and juice of 1 lime

1 carrot, diced

1 courgette, diced

2 large shallots, diced

1 fennel bulb, diced

1 bunch watercress

Salt and freshly ground black pepper

Serves 4

Pour the white wine into a large pan and add the mussels and clams. Cover and cook on a high heat for about 5 minutes until the shells have opened. Drain the mussels and clams, reserving the liquid. Shell the mussels and clams, discarding any that remain closed.

Return the liquid to the pan. Bring to the boil and reduce by half. Mix in the olive oil and lime zest and juice. Add the vegetables, reduce the heat and simmer for about 5 minutes, or until the vegetables are tender.

Add the watercress, mussels and clams and reheat gently. Season to taste and serve immediately.

Mussels are child's play to cook. Try this oriental take on the traditional mussels in cream sauce.

steamed mussels

with lemongrass, ginger and coconut

you will need

2 tbsp olive oil

3 cloves garlic, crushed

4 shallots, finely chopped

2 stalks lemongrass

5cm/2in root ginger, peeled and finely chopped

250g/8oz leeks, chopped

125g/4oz carrots, chopped

250g/8oz celery, chopped

1 sprig thyme

1 sprig rosemary

1kg/2lb mussels, scrubbed and rinsed, with beards removed

300ml/½ pint white wine

1 litre/1¾ pints Fish Stock

75ml/3fl oz coconut milk

100ml/3½fl oz single cream

Salt and freshly ground black pepper

2 tbsp chopped coriander

Serves 4

Heat the olive oil in a large pan over gentle heat. Add the garlic, shallots, lemongrass, ginger, leeks, carrots and celery. Cover and sweat for 5–6 minutes or until soft. Add the thyme and rosemary and transfer to a bowl. Rinse out the pan.

Put the mussels, white wine and fish stock in the pan over a high heat. Cover and steam for about 5 minutes or until the mussels open. Remove the mussels with a slotted spoon and place in a large serving dish, discarding any mussels that have not opened.

Add the vegetables to the cooking liquid, bring to the boil and cook until reduced by half. Stir in the coconut milk and cream and adjust the seasoning. Add the chopped coriander and pour over the mussels.

Chillies and garlic give these mussels a punch. Serve with crusty French bread, or the Basil Bread (see page 154).

steamed mussels

with garlic, coriander and chilli

Heat the olive oil in a pan over low heat. Add the garlic, chillies, shallots, ginger, leeks, and celery. Cover and sweat for 5-6 minutes or until soft. Add the thyme and rosemary and transfer to a bowl. Rinse out the pan.

Place the mussels, white wine and fish stock in the pan over high heat. Cover and steam for about 5 minutes, or until the mussels open. Remove the mussels with a slotted spoon and place in a serving dish, discarding any that have not opened.

Add the vegetables to the pan. Bring to the boil and cook until reduced by half. Remove from the heat, stir in the cream and adjust the seasoning. Add the chopped herbs and pour over the mussels to serve.

you will need

2 tbsp olive oil

4 cloves garlic, crushed

2 chillies, deseeded and sliced

4 shallots, chopped

25g/1oz root ginger, peeled chopped

3 leeks, chopped

1 stick of celery, chopped

1 sprig thyme

1 sprig rosemary

1kg/2lb mussels, scrubbed and rinsed, with beards removed

300ml/½ pint white wine

1 litre/1¾ pints Fish Stock

100ml/3½fl oz double cream

Salt and freshly ground black pepper

50g/2oz fresh coriander leaves, chopped

50g/2oz fresh flat-leaf parsley, chopped

Serves 4

gnocchi

These traditional Italian dumplings make a wonderful accompaniment to grilled meats or pasta with sauces.

Place the potatoes in a bowl and make a well in the centre. Add the polenta and egg yolks and mix into a dough, then mix in the flour. Season with salt and pepper and mix in the chives and thyme.

Roll the dough into a sausage shape, then cut into 2.5cm/1in pieces. Bring a large pan of water to the boil. Add the gnocchi and simmer for 1 minute. They will float to the top when ready. Remove with a slotted spoon and drain on kitchen paper.

you will need

1kg/2lb hot mashed potatoes

1 tbsp polenta

5 egg yolks

3 tbsp flour

Salt and freshly ground black pepper

2 tbsp chopped chives

1 tsp finely chopped thyme

Serves 4

For a really spectacular presentation, use deep-fried strips of aubergine skin to make a flamboyant garnish, as shown below.

crab salad

with avocado cream

To make the avocado cream, blend the avocado flesh with the crème fraîche and half the lemon juice until smooth. Season well and pour the remaining lemon juice on top. Chill until ready to serve.

Bring a large pan of water to the boil. Add the crabs and cook for 6 minutes, then plunge into cold water. Remove the flesh and mix with the crème fraîche, lemon juice and herbs. Season and chill. Mix most of the vinaigrette with the vegetables and marinate for 10 minutes.

To serve, place a pastry cutter on each plate and spoon in the vegetables and crabmeat. Stir the lemon juice into the avocado cream, then spoon onto each salad. Carefully remove the rings. Garnish with tomato, grapefruit segments and mint leaves and drizzle with the remaining vinaigrette around the bottom of the salad.

you will need

4 uncooked blue swimmer crabs

3 tbsp crème fraîche

2 tbsp lemon juice

2 tsp finely chopped mint

1 tsp finely chopped tarragon

Salt and freshly ground black pepper

Lemongrass vinaigrette (see page 154)

2 carrots, finely sliced

2 turnips, finely diced

Tomato quarters, pink grapefruit segments and mint leaves, to garnish

AVOCADO CREAM

2 large avocados

2 tbsp crème fraîche

Juice of 2 lemons

Serves 6

ravioli of goat's cheese

In a bowl mix the goat's cheese, cream cheese and the herbs. Mould the mixture into little balls and place in the fridge.

Roll out the pasta dough using a pasta machine or rolling pin. Divide the sheet into 2 rectangles and keep one sheet covered with a clean tea towel or clingfilm while you work with the other. Using 10cm/4 in and 12cm/5 in pastry cutters, cut out 2 discs of each size. Place one ball of filling in the centre of each smaller disc, brush the edges with beaten egg and top with a larger disc. Press the edges to seal. Repeat with the other rectangle. Blanch the ravioli for 1 minute in hot salted water and rinse under cold water. Coat with olive oil and cover with clingfilm until ready to serve.

you will need

500g/1lb goat's cheese

100g/3½ oz cream cheese

20 coriander leaves, chopped

20 flat-leaf parsley leaves, chopped

20 chives, chopped

1 recipe Pasta Dough (see page 123)

1 egg, beaten

Olive oil

Serves 4

steamed cod on a warm salad
with champagne vinaigrette

you will need

150ml/¼ pint olive oil

4 tbsp Champagne Vinaigrette (see page 154)

2 red onions, diced

1/2 cucumber, cut into 1cm/½ in dice

500g/1lb new potatoes, boiled

Salt and freshly ground black pepper

4 x 150g/5oz cod fillets

Serves 4

To make the potato salad, heat the olive oil and 3 tablespoons of the vinaigrette in a pan over a low heat. Add the red onion and cucumber and heat gently for 2 minutes. Add the new potatoes, season with salt and pepper and transfer to a dish to keep warm. Rinse out the pan.

Half-fill the pan with boiling water. Place the cod fillets in a steamer over the pan and steam for 4 minutes. Arrange some potato salad on each plate and place a cod fillet on top. Drizzle with the remaining champagne vinaigrette.

I first tasted cappuccino soup eleven years ago, in a 3-star restaurant in France. The soup has been on the menu at Peacock Alley for five years now, and has become one of its trademarks. You do need a frying pan as well.

cappuccino of haricots

with morels and seared scallops

you will need

250g/8oz dried haricot beans, soaked overnight

Salt

1 small onion, peeled

1 carrot, peeled

1 sprig thyme

1 sprig rosemary

800ml/1 pint 7fl oz Chicken or Vegetable Stock

(see page 153)

25g/1oz butter

100g/3½ oz morels

1–2 tsp truffle oil

150ml/¼ pint double cream

50g/2oz butter, diced and chilled

1 tbsp olive oil

4 scallops

Tarragon leaves, to garnish

sliced chillies, to garnish

Bread sticks, to serve

Serves 4

Drain the beans, transfer to a large pan and add enough lightly salted cold water to cover by 5cm/2 in. Add the onion, carrot and herbs. Bring to a boil, boil for 10 minutes then lower the heat to a simmer. Cook for 25–30 minutes until soft. Drain and discard the onion, carrot and herbs. In a processor, blend the beans to a fine purée. Rinse out the pan.

Place the stock in the pan and cook for 5 minutes over a high heat until reduced. Meanwhile, melt 25g/1oz of the butter in a frying pan and sauté the mushrooms for 2–3 minutes. Sprinkle with a little of the truffle oil. Transfer to a bowl and wipe out the pan with kitchen paper.

Using a hand-held blender, mix the bean purée into the reduced stock until smooth, then whisk in the cream and remaining truffle oil. Divide the mushrooms between 4 cups. Reheat the soup and add the cold butter. Whisk with the hand-held blender until the mixture bubbles.

Heat the olive oil in the frying pan and sauté the scallops for 1 minute on each side. Pour the soup into the cups and place a skewered scallop on the side of each cup. Garnish with tarragon leaves and sliced chillies and serve with bread sticks.

This may be a bit of a cholesterol special, but if you don't care, please eat it!

spaghetti carbonara

with peas and poached eggs

you will need

1 tbsp malt vinegar

8 eggs

3 tbsp olive oil

500g/1lb dried spaghetti

200g/7oz smoked streaky bacon, cut
into thick 1cm/½in pieces

200g/7oz peas

Salt and freshly ground black pepper

2 tbsp crème fraiche

2 tbsp finely chopped parsley

90g/3oz freshly grated Parmesan

Serves 4

Quarter-fill a pan with boiling water and bring to a gentle simmer over a medium heat. Add the vinegar, stirring the water to make a whirlpool, crack 2 eggs into the centre of the pan and allow to cook for 1–2 minutes. Remove from the pan with a slotted spoon and drain on kitchen paper. Repeat with another 2 eggs. Transfer the eggs to a bowl of cold water.

Fill the pan with salted water and bring to the boil. Add 1 tablespoon of olive oil and cook the spaghetti until al dente. Drain well and rinse with plenty of cold water. Drain again, drizzle with more olive oil, then transfer to a bowl.

Bring the pan to the boil again with salted water and add the peas. Cook for 3–4 minutes and refresh under cold water. Drain well. Rinse out the pan.

Heat the remaining olive oil in the pan and cook the bacon over a medium heat for 5–6 minutes until crispy. Add black pepper and cook for 1 minute. Add the spaghetti and peas and toss until warmed through. Mix together the remaining eggs, crème fraîche and parsley and add to the pan. Remove from the heat and stir constantly for 1 minute to allow the heat to cook the eggs.

To serve, stir in half the Parmesan and place the poached eggs on top of the spaghetti. Sprinkle with the remaining Parmesan to garnish.

shallow pan

The shallow pan is very versatile, suitable for many recipes. It allows you to prepare dishes such as ratatouille quickly. as all the vegetables are evenly spread over the heat source. I can stress enough that the better the quality of your pan, the better the results. The ideal shallow pan has a large, round base of copper or steel. You can fry, stew or poach with this pan.

For those who are bored with the more traditional ways of serving asparagus, this gives it a new twist without involving too much work.

provençal asparagus

you will need

25g/1oz butter

1 shallot, finely diced

2 cloves garlic, crushed

1 sprig thyme

1 sprig rosemary

50ml/2fl oz Chicken Stock (see page 153)

Salt and freshly ground black pepper

24 asparagus spears, peeled and
blanched for 1 minute

Small bunch of chives, finely chopped

Serves 4

Melt the butter in a large shallow pan over moderate heat Add the shallot, garlic and herbs, cover and sweat gently for 3–4 minutes without allowing it to colour. Add the chicken stock, season well, and reduce the heat to a gentle simmer. Add the asparagus for about 30 seconds, until heated through. Add the chopped chives just before serving.

This is an unusual recipe in that the ratatouille is quite dry, not like the usual stew of vegetables. Serve it with couscous or rice dishes.

ratatouille

with rocket and parmesan

you will need

2 tbsp olive oil

2 shallots, chopped

4 cloves garlic, crushed

2 red peppers, deseeded and finely diced

1 yellow pepper, deseeded and finely diced

4 courgettes, finely diced

2 aubergines, finely diced

100g/3½oz tomato purée

2 tsp sugar

Salt and freshly ground black pepper

2 tbsp white wine

1 tbsp finely chopped basil

200g/7oz rocket

4 tbsp Balsamic Vinaigrette (see page 154)

25g/1oz Parmesan, shaved

Serves 4

Heat the oil in a pan. Add the shallots and garlic, cover and sweat over gentle heat until soft.

Add all the vegetables and cook quickly over a high heat. Add the tomato purée and cook for 1–2 minutes, stirring frequently. Season with sugar, salt and pepper. Deglaze with white wine and add the basil.

Toss the rocket with the vinaigrette. To serve, spoon the ratatouille into a ring, dress with the salad, season and garnish with Parmesan shavings.

Up to five years ago any monkfish caught in Irish waters would have been thrown back, or used as bait. Now it is very expensive, and will be almost extinct in another five years.

medallion of monkfish

with soy and choy sum

Blanch the choy sum in a pan of boiling, salted water for 3 minutes and refresh under cold water. Drain well. Rinse out the pan.

Combine the lemon juice, garlic, grated ginger and soy sauce in a bowl.

Place the oil in the pan over a high heat and cook the monkfish for 1 minute on each side. Add the choy sum, carrot and spring onions, and the garlic mixture. Increase the heat and add the butter. Swirl the pan to incorporate the butter, season well and sprinkle with the chilli strips. Serve iimmediately.

you will need

1kg/2lb choy sum, shredded

Salt and freshly ground black pepper

Juice of 1 lemon

5 cloves garlic, crushed

2.5cm/1in root ginger, peeled and grated

2 tbsp sweet soy sauce

1 tbsp olive oil

1kg/2lb monkfish fillets, cut into 12 medallions

1 carrot, cut into thin strips

4 spring onions, cut into thin strips

50g/2oz butter, cubed

1 large red chilli pepper, deseeded and cut into strips

Serves 4

This is the perfect way of eating chocolate. The dish is rich but light, with none of that heavy chocolatey feeling.

hazelnut praline

you will need

150ml/¼ pint single cream

100g/3½ oz white chocolate

100g/3½ oz hazelnut nougat
(available in specialist shops)

2 tsp paté noisette
(available in specialist shops)

1 gelatine leaf, soaked in a small
amount of water

250ml/8fl oz whipping cream,
lightly whipped

Ice-cream and chocolate curls,
to serve

Finely chopped hazelnuts, to decorate

Serves 4

Put the cream in a pan and bring to the boil. Boil for 1-2 minutes, then add the white chocolate. When it starts to melt mix in the nougat and pate noisette. Take off the heat and allow to cool slightly, then add the gelatine as the mixture starts to cool down.

Fold in the whipped cream. Pour into dariole moulds and freeze until set. To remove from the moulds, dip the base in boiling water for 10 seconds and then invert on to a plate. Serve with vanilla, chocolate or white chocolate ice-cream and chocolate curls. Sprinkle with finely chopped hazelnuts.

The perfect light dessert to end a heavy, rich meal – and it looks so beautiful.

poached pears in vanilla

with fromage blanc sorbet

Place all the syrup ingredients in a pan over low heat until sugar is dissolved. When all the sugar has dissolved completely, boil for 30 minutes. Let it cool to 75°C.

Add the pears and cook for 30 minutes on a low heat until the syrup has reduced to half. Transfer the pears to a shallow dish and strain the syrup over them. Wash out the pan.

For the sorbet, place the water, glucose, trimouline and lemon juice in the pan and bring to the boil. Let the mixture cool and then add the fromage blanc. Process in a ice-cream machine for about 40 minutes or freeze in a plastic container.

To serve, arrange each pear in the centre of a large plate and decorate with a mint sprig. Pour some syrup around the pear and serve with a scoop of sorbet.

you will need

4 large, firm pears, peeled and cored, but left whole

Mint sprigs, to decorate

SYRUP

500g/1lb caster sugar

1 litre/1¾ pints water

3 vanilla pods

Peel of 1 orange

Peel of 1 lemon

1 tsp rose-water

1 star anise

1 clove

FROMAGE BLANC SORBET

500ml/17fl oz water

80g/3oz glucose

25g/1oz trimouline

4 tbsp lemon juice

500g/1lb fromage blanc

Serves 4

The humble stewed apple is transformed when it is cooked with spices and served with vanilla-flavoured crème fraîche

stewed apple with cinnamon

five spice, crème fraîche and vanilla

Place the lemon juice in a bowl, add the chopped apples and roll them in the lemon juice to avoid discoloration.

you will need

Juice of 1 lemon

7 golden delicious or Granny Smith apples, peeled, cored and chopped

45g/1½oz unsalted butter

1 cinnamon stick

1 tbsp five-spice powder

6 tbsp sugar

6 tbsp ground almonds

4 large tbsp crème fraîche

1 vanilla pod

Serves 4

Heat a pan over medium heat and add half the butter. Add the apple, cinnamon and five-spice powder and cook for 8 minutes. Add the sugar and sprinkle with the ground almonds. Cook for a further 20 minutes on a medium heat.

Mix the crème fraîche with the seeds from the vanilla pod. Serve the apples with a spoonful of crème fraîche.

frying pan

Frying pans have come in for a lot of bad press in recent years – own one, and your cholesterol level is obviously not a concern. But the recipes in this chapter do not involve large quantities of oil and fat. Non-stick frying pans with thick cast-iron or copper bases allow you to fry with little fat, as the heat is evenly spread over the pan.

Scallops are my favourite ingredient, hence there are a lot of scallop dishes in this book. In my spare time I go diving, hand-picking scallops off the coast of Cork and Donegal – they taste much better than the dredged ones.

seared scallops

with guacamole, coriander and chilli

you will need

1 avocado

Juice of 1 lemon

Juice of 1 lime

Salt and freshly ground black pepper

50g/2oz coriander leaves, chopped

1 clove garlic, chopped

1 chilli, deseeded and diced

50g/2oz chives, chopped

1 tbsp olive oil

25g/1oz butter

12 fresh scallops

2 tbsp coconut milk

coriander sprigs, to garnish

AVOCADO SALAD

1 avocado, diced

1 chilli, deseeded and diced

30g/1½oz coriander leaves, chopped

Serves 4

Peel and stone the avocado and dice finely. Place in a small bowl, add the lemon and lime juice and season with salt and pepper. Process the coriander, garlic, chilli and chives in a food processor, then mix in with the avocado.

Heat the olive oil and butter in a small frying pan. Season the scallops then sear for 1 minute on each side. Mix the ingredients for the salad in a bowl. Serve the scallops with spoonfuls of guacamole and avocado salad.

Creamy, fresh-tasting pea purée and crispy pancetta look wonderfully colourful and add a new dimension to the deep-sea flavour of the scallops.

seared scallops

with crispy pancetta and pea purée

Heat half the butter in a large frying pan over gentle heat, add the shallots, cover and sweat until just starting to soften. Add the peas and cook for 1 minute before adding the sugar, seasoning and cream. Bring to the boil, then cook gently for about 15 minutes until the cream has reduced.

you will need

100g/3½oz butter

2 shallots, roughly chopped

250g/8oz fresh or frozen peas

1 teaspoon caster sugar

Salt and freshly ground black pepper

150ml/¼ pint double cream

Juice of 1 lemon

12–20 scallops, depending on
  whether or not this is a starter or
  main course

8 thin slices pancetta

Salad leaves, to serve

Flat-leaf parsley, to garnish

Serves 4

Purée the mixture in a food processor and if the mixture is not thick enough return to the frying pan and cook gently until it has thickened slightly. Season with the lemon juice and transfer to a serving dish. Keep warm.

Rinse out the pan and heat the remaining butter on a high heat. Season the scallops well and sear on both sides for about 30–40 seconds. Add the pancetta and cook for another 1–2 minutes until the pancetta is crispy.

To serve, arrange the scallops on each plate with a slice of pancetta. Top with some salad leaves and another slice of pancetta, and finish with a spoonful of pea purée. Garnish with sprigs of flat-leaf parsley.

My favourite ingredient again! Quick, easy and delicious, these seared scallops make the ideal starter. Try to get fresh ones – the frozen variety tend to be very watery.

seared scallops

with rocket and parmesan salad

Heat the oil in a frying pan. Season the scallops and fry for 1 minute on each side until golden. Turn off the heat and keep the scallops warm.

Mix the rocket with the Parmesan shavings in a salad bowl. Add the vinaigrette, the scallops and their juices. Toss the salad to coat everything well in the vinaigrette and serve immediately.

you will need

2 tbsp groundnut oil

Salt and freshly ground black pepper

12 scallops

4 handfuls rocket leaves

125g/4oz Parmesan,
shaved or grated

1 recipe quantity Balsamic
Vinaigrette (see page 154)

Serves 4

capellini cakes

you will need

200g/7oz capellini or angel hair pasta, soaked
in boiling water until al dente

90ml/3fl oz olive oil

50g/2oz butter

2 tbsp finely grated Parmesan

Salt and freshly ground black pepper

Serves 4

Drain the pasta and toss in a large bowl with 4 tablespoons of the olive oil, the butter and Parmesan. Season well. Arrange the pasta in 4 x 8cm/3½in metal rings. Heat the remaining olive oil in a large frying pan. Using a fish slice, transfer the rings to the pan and sauté the pasta gently for 1–2 minutes on both sides.

Finish by grilling the pasta cakes under low heat for 2–3 minutes until crispy. Serve the cakes immediately, with grilled meat or chicken.

pan-fried squid
with chilli

Slit the squid down one side and lay them out flat. Make small criss-cross cuts in the squid, using a sharp knife. Mix half the olive oil, garlic, chilli and lemon juice in a bowl and add the squid. Turn to coat and leave to marinate for 15 minutes.

Heat a large frying pan until smoking, then add the remaining oil. Drain the squid, reserving the marinade, and put in the pan. Season with salt and pepper. Toss the squid in the pan for about 3 minutes, then add the reserved marinade and the chopped parsley. Mix well and serve immediately.

you will need

1kg/2lb baby squid

3 tbsp olive oil

1 clove garlic, crushed

1 red chilli, deseeded and finely chopped

Juice of 1 lemon

Salt and freshly ground black pepper

Handful of flat-leaf parsley, chopped

Serves 4

I hadn't cooked omelettes in years, until my daughter went through an omelette phase while we were trying to get some protein into her. This is her favourite.

crab omelette

with braised spring onions and coriander

Melt one-third of the butter in a frying pan and sauté the spring onions for a few minutes. Season and add the sugar. Add a few tablespoons of water if they start to burn, and allow the water to evaporate. When they are just wilted, remove from the pan and keep warm. Wipe the pan clean with kitchen paper.

Mix the cream and crabmeat together and season well. Place the olive oil in the pan over moderate heat with half the remaining butter. Whisk the eggs and season well. Dice the remaining butter and add to the egg mixture.

Pour the eggs into the frying pan and swirl around, drawing the outside to the centre with a wooden spatula and allowing the liquid to set. Turn the heat low and spoon the crab mixture and half the coriander into the centre. Fold over the sides of the omelette and gently slide onto a plate. Sprinkle with chopped coriander and serve with the warm spring onions and a green salad.

you will need

300g/10oz butter

16 spring onions, trimmed

Salt and freshly ground black pepper

2 tsp caster sugar

100ml/3½ fl oz double cream

300g/10oz fresh crabmeat

3 tbsp olive oil

12 eggs

3 tbsp chopped coriander

Green salad, to serve

Serves 4

This recipe cheats slightly by using two pans – you will need a saucepan to cook the tagliatelle and heat the sauce – but I hope you agree the end result is worth the extra washing up.

roasted monkfish

with tagliatelle and cream

you will need

500g/1lb tagliatelle

Salt and freshly ground black pepper

100ml/3¼ fl oz olive oil

4 x 175g/6oz fillets of monkfish

500ml/17fl oz double cream

1 clove garlic, crushed

4 tbsp chopped fresh sage

Serves 4

Preheat the oven to 200°C/400°F/Gas mark 6.

Boil the tagliatelle in a large pan of boiling, salted water until al dente. Drain, rinse under cold water and drain again. Toss the tagliatelle in half the olive oil and set aside. Rinse out the pan.

Heat the remaining olive oil in a large ovenproof frying pan. Season the monkfish with plenty of salt and pepper and sear on all sides for 2–3 minutes. Transfer to the oven to finish cooking for 7 minutes.

Place the cream, garlic and sage in the large pan and bring to the boil. Season well and cook until reduced slightly. Add the tagliatelle and toss well. Serve with the monkfish.

Wild salmon are in season in Ireland from June to August. During these months I go fishing every Sunday, from Blessington in County Wicklow to Lough Foyle.

roasted salmon

with saffron cream sauce

you will need

4 x 175g/6oz salmon fillets, skinned and boned

2 tbsp vegetable oil

Salt and freshly ground white pepper

500g/1lb spinach, precooked in a little butter, drained and kept warm

1 knob of butter

12 Gnocchi (see page 33)

SAFFRON CREAM SAUCE

200g/7oz unsalted butter, chilled and diced

2 shallots, chopped

1 clove garlic, crushed

250ml/8fl oz dry white wine

100ml/3½ fl oz whipping cream

Pinch of saffron

Serves 4

First make the sauce. Melt half the butter in a deep heavy frying pan and add the shallots and garlic. Cover and sweat over moderate heat until soft. Add the white wine and boil until the sauce has reduced to 4 tablespoons. Pour in the cream, add the saffron and boil again for 1 minute. Start to whisk in the remaining butter, a cube at a time, and continue to whisk until the butter is well incorporated. Season with salt and pepper and remove from the heat. Pour the sauce into a jug and keep warm. Wash out the pan.

Cut the salmon fillets into 4 even slices and season with salt and pepper. Heat the vegetable oil in the frying pan over medium heat. Place the salmon in the pan and cook for 4 minutes, then turn and cook for 3 more minutes. This will cook the salmon to a golden brown. Meanwhile, reheat the spinach in a small pan with a knob of butter, season and drain.

To serve, spoon the sauce on to each plate. Arrange 3 gnocchi on the plate, and place the salmon slices in the centre with the spinach carefully placed on top.

Another elegant stuffed omelette, this time with a Thai flavour, using garlic, coriander and fish sauce to give an intriguing piquancy to the stuffing.

omelette stuffed

with minced pork

Heat a large frying pan and add 2 tablespoons of the oil. Add the garlic and sweat over gentle heat until golden, then add the onion. Cook for 1 minute, then add the pork and stir-fry for 6–8 minutes. Stir in the fish sauce, then add the tomatoes and sugar. Simmer until the sauce begins to thicken, then remove from the heat and stir in the chopped coriander. Season the mixture and transfer to a bowl. Wipe the pan clean with kitchen paper.

Beat the eggs in a bowl with the water. Heat the frying pan over moderate heat and add the remaining oil. Pour in the eggs and roll around until the surface of the pan is covered. Cook until the egg is almost cooked through, then remove from the heat. Spoon the pork mixture across the centre of the egg and fold either side over the filling. Tip the omelette onto a large plate and sprinkle with coriander leaves.

you will need

5 tbsp vegetable oil

4 cloves garlic, crushed

1 small onion, finely chopped

250g/8oz minced pork

2 tsp fish sauce (nam pla)

125g/4oz cherry tomatoes,
    quartered

2 tsp caster sugar

2 tbsp chopped coriander

Salt and freshly ground black
pepper

6 eggs

1 tsp water

Coriander leaves, to garnish

Serves 4

The rich sweetness of the beetroot confit goes well with the slightly gamey flavour of guinea fowl, now widely available.

roasted guinea fowl

with confit of beetroot

Preheat the oven to 200°C/400°F/Gas mark 6.

you will need

100ml/3½fl oz olive oil

1 free-range guinea fowl, cut into 6 joints

4 cooked beetroot, peeled and cubed

2 tbsp red wine vinegar

5 sprigs thyme

200ml/7fl oz water

Salt and freshly ground black pepper

Serves 4

Heat half the oil in a large ovenproof frying pan and sear the guinea fowl joints for 4 minutes on each side. Add the beetroot, vinegar, thyme and water. Season well. Transfer the pan to the preheated oven and roast for 30 minutes.

Remove the guinea fowl pieces with a slotted spoon and place on a large serving dish, allowing the juices to drain into the beetroot. Place the pan on top of the stove on a high heat, to allow the water to evaporate. Add the remaining olive oil, season well and serve with the guinea fowl.

Fillet of beef is the best cut meat that you can buy, renowned for its exquisite tenderness. It is often served with equally luxurious accompaniments, but braised endive gives a lighter, more modern touch.

peppered beef fillet

with braised endive

Mix the marinade ingredients in a shallow dish. Add the beef, turn to coat and leave to marinate for 2–3 hours.

Heat the olive oil in a large frying pan over a high heat. Add the endive, flat sides down and char for a few minutes. Add the butter and sprinkle on the caster sugar. Season well and when the mixture starts to caramelise turn down the heat. Add a few tablespoons of water, and turn the endive so they cook on both sides. Turn up the heat and when they are golden and starting to caramelise transfer to a warm place.

Wipe the pan clean with kitchen paper. Drain the beef and heat 2 tablespoons of the marinade in the pan. Add the beef and sear on both sides over a very high heat, about 3–4 minutes for medium rare.

Allow to rest for a minute, then serve with the endive and drizzle with aïoli.

you will need

4 fillets of beef, about 200g/7oz each

50ml/2fl oz olive oil

4 heads endive, sliced in half lengthways

100g/3½oz butter

3 tsp caster sugar

Salt and freshly ground black pepper

Aïoli, to serve

MARINADE

100ml/3½fl oz olive oil

2 tbsp coarse ground black pepper

2 tsp rock salt

2 tsp Worcestershire sauce

Serves 4

I have been a big fan of maple syrup ever since I lived in the States. It has the same effect as honey, but with a much more distinctive flavour.

maple-glazed pears

with spiced cream

Whip the cream with the cardamom and icing sugar, then refrigerate until ready to serve.

you will need

300ml/½ pint double cream

½ teaspoon ground cardamom

1 tbsp icing sugar

50g/2oz butter

4 pears, cored, peeled and sliced into

quarters

4 tbsp maple syrup

Serves 4

Melt the butter in a large frying pan over a medium heat. Add the pears and sauté for 2–3 minutes. Add the maple syrup and gently turn the pears so that they become slightly caramelised on all sides.

Remove from the heat and allow to cool. Serve with spoonfuls of the spiced cream.

sauté pan

If you only have one pan in your kitchen cupboard, make it a sauté pan. It should be made of lined copper, but stainless steel is more common. The wider the pan, the better, and it should have low sides to allow steam to escape. The lid is optional, but it does help in some recipes which require a lot of heat. If the handles are also steel, the sauté pan can be transferred to the oven to finish off the cooking.

This dish was first cooked in the restaurant by Steve Brewer, a close friend whose passion both for foie gras and cooking goes beyond anything.

brewer's foie gras

Season the foie gras and place in a sauté pan over high heat. Sear on both sides then remove from the heat and reserve. Rinse out the pan.

you will need

4 x 90g/3½oz slices of foie gras

Salt and freshly ground black pepper

600ml/1 pint water

2 tbsp orange-blossom water

60g/2¼oz sugar

2 tbsp lemon juice

2 tbsp orange juice

1 vanilla pod

24 orange segments

25g/1oz butter, cut into knobs

Watercress, to serve

Sliced chillies, to serve

Deep-fried salsify strips, to garnish (optional)

Serves 4

Make a syrup by placing the water, orange-blossom water, sugar, lemon juice and orange juice in the pan. Add the vanilla pod and cook for 8–10 minutes. Strain the syrup through a sieve into a bowl, removing the vanilla pod. Split the pod, scrape out the seeds and add them to the syrup. Rinse out the pan.

Return the foie gras to the pan and sauté over moderate heat until golden brown. Add the orange segments. Pour in the syrup and cook until it has reduced to a thick sauce. When ready to serve, add the butter.

To serve, sprinkle with watercress and sliced chilli. Garnish with strips of deep-fried salsify, if using.

A dramatic presentation using the aptly named trompettes de mort lifts a simple pasta dish out of the ordinary.

Linguine

with trompettes de mort

Fill a large sauté pan with water, add 2 tablespoons of the olive oil and bring to the boil. Add the linguine and cook for about 8 minutes, or until al dente. Drain, refresh in ice-cold water and store in the fridge on a tray until ready to serve.

Heat 1 tablespoon of the oil in the sauté pan, add the trompettes and sweat over a gentle heat for 2–3 minutes. Remove from the pan and reserve.

Heat the remaining oil in the pan, add the shallots, garlic and dried mushrooms and sweat over gentle heat until the shallots and garlic are softened but not coloured. Add the chicken stock, increase the heat and simmer until reduced by half. Add the cream and again simmer until reduced by half. Add the pasta to the sauce, season well and heat through gently.

Serve the linguine in the sauce, sprinkled with chopped chervil, and arrange some trompettes on each serving.

you will need

4 tbsp olive oil

175g/6oz dried linguine

125g/4oz fresh trompettes de mort

4 shallots, finely sliced

2 cloves garlic, finely sliced

25g/1oz mixed dried mushrooms,
soaked in warm water for 20
minutes and drained

600ml/1 pint Chicken Stock
(see page 153)

150ml/¼ pint double cream

Salt and freshly ground black
pepper

2 tbsp chopped fresh chervil

Serves 4

Don't worry if you don't possess a sauté pan – these delicious Chinese-style prawns could also be cooked in a frying pan or a wok.

pan-fried prawns

with chilli, ginger, coriander and bok choy

Heat a large sauté pan and pour in the sesame oil. Add the garlic, chillies and ginger and sauté for about 30 seconds over a high heat.

you will need

2 tbsp sesame oil

1 clove garlic, diced

1 red chilli, deseeded and diced

1 green chilli, deseeded and diced

2.5cm/1in root ginger, peeled and finely diced

1kg/2lb large raw prawns, shelled and deveined

1kg/2lb bok choy, leaves separated

1 tbsp honey

2 tbsp soy sauce

Juice of 1 lime

Salt and freshly ground black pepper

Coriander leaves, to garnish

Serves 4

Place the prawns in the pan with the bok choy and sauté for 1 minute. Add the honey, soy sauce and lime juice. Simmer for 1 minute, season and serve sprinkled with coriander leaves.

My favourite ingredient again, this time teamed with caramelised apples and sauté potatoes to give a combination of flavours that is quite irresistible.

scallops

with caramelised apples and sauté potatoes

Heat the oil in a large sauté pan over moderate heat. Add the potato slices and sauté until tender and golden brown. Remove the potatoes with a slotted spoon and keep warm.

Add the scallops to the hot pan and sauté for about 1 minute on one side and 30 seconds on the other side. Remove with a slotted spoon and keep warm.

Sprinkle the apples with the caster sugar and add to the pan over a high heat. Pour in the cider and white wine and boil until reduced by half. Remove the apples with a slotted spoon and add the chicken stock. Bring back to the boil and reduce by half.

Return the potatoes, scallops and apples to the pan and cook for another minute. Season with salt and pepper and serve while hot.

you will need

4 large baking potatoes, cut into
5mm/¼in thick slices

3 tbsp olive oil

8 large scallops, sliced in half

4 Granny Smith apples, peeled, cored and chopped

3 tbsp caster sugar

3 tbsp cider

3 tbsp white wine

100ml/3½ fl oz Chicken Stock (see page 153)

Salt and freshly ground black pepper

Serves 4

Pasta ribbons and oyster mushrooms in a creamy mustard sauce are the perfect accompaniment for tender rabbit loin.

pappardelle with rabbit loin,

mustard and parsley

Cook the pappardelle in a large sauté pan of boiling salted water until al dente. Drain and reserve. Rinse out the pan.

you will need

125g/4oz dried pappardelle

Salt and freshly ground black pepper

50g/2oz butter

8 rabbit loins

2 shallots, diced

1 clove garlic, diced

10 oyster mushrooms

150ml/¼ pint white wine

300ml/½ pint Chicken Stock (see page 153)

1 tbsp wholegrain mustard

1 tbsp double cream

1 tbsp chopped flat-leaf parsley

10–12 blanched spinach leaves (optional)

Serves 4

Heat half the butter in the pan over moderate heat. Season the rabbit and sauté for about 10 minutes on each side, or until cooked through, then remove from the pan and keep warm.

Add the remaining butter to the pan and sauté the shallots, garlic and oyster mushrooms for 2 minutes. Add the white wine and bring to the boil, reducing the mixture by half, then add the stock and reduce again. Add the rabbit, mustard and cream and mix in the pappardelle. Allow to simmer for 3 minutes, until the pasta is heated through. Add the chopped parsley and season to taste.

For an optional presentation, as shown here, take half the cooked rabbit and cut into medallions. Wrap the rabbit pieces in blanched spinach leaves, return to the pan and warm through.

Puy lentils, richly flavoured with smoked bacon, garlic and onions, are the perfect foil to tender slices of calf's liver. The final addition of balsamic vinegar enhances the rich taste.

calf's liver and bacon

with puy lentils

Pour the oil into a large sauté pan over a moderately high heat. Season the liver and seal in the hot oil on both sides, then remove from the pan and keep warm.

Add the smoked bacon, garlic and onions to the pan and sauté until golden brown. Drain the lentils and add to the pan with the chicken stock. Leave to simmer for 1½–2 hours.

Return the liver to the pan and cook with the lentils for another 10 minutes. Mix in the balsamic vinegar and serve sprinkled with chopped parsley.

you will need

4 tbsp olive oil

Salt and freshly ground black pepper

400g/13oz calf's liver, sliced

200g/7oz smoked bacon, cut into strips

2 cloves garlic, crushed

20 baby onions

100g/3½oz Puy lentils, soaked for 24 hours

600ml/1 pint Chicken Stock (see page 153)

4 tbsp balsamic vinegar

4 tbsp chopped parsley

Serves 4

Fresh ceps are among the best of all mushrooms, with a deep, rich flavour. Sautéed with fresh herbs and cream, they taste divine.

sautéed ceps with wild rocket,

thyme, rosemary and cream

Cook the penne in a large sauté pan of boiling salted water for about 8 minutes,until al dente, then drain and transfer to a bowl. Rinse out the pan.

Melt the butter in the pan over moderate heat and sauté the ceps, shallots and garlic for 3 minutes. Add the pasta and mix thoroughly. Pour in the chicken stock and simmer for 1 minute. Add the rosemary and thyme, simmer for a further minute and pour in the cream. Bring to the boil and season.

Add the rocket at the last minute. Toss well and serve.

you will need

500g/1lb dried penne

Salt and freshly ground black pepper

50g/2oz butter

250g/8oz fresh ceps, trimmed

2 shallots, diced

1 clove garlic, diced

200ml/7fl oz Chicken Stock (see page 153)

1 sprig rosemary, chopped

2 springs thyme, chopped

150g/5oz double cream

2 bunches rocket

Serves 4

casserole dish

For these recipes you need a casserole dish that is equally happy on top of the stove or in the oven, so the bottom should be thick and heavy enough to withstand the heat. The most popular makes are usually cast-iron, sometimes lined with enamel, and should last a lifetime with careful use.

The baby aubergines were char-grilled for a more dramatic presentation, but they could be cooked in the casserole with the chicken, if preferred.

thai green curry

with baby aubergines and sticky rice

you will need

1 chicken, cut into 6 joints

Salt and freshly ground black pepper

3 tbsp olive oil

250ml/8fl oz Chicken Stock (see page 153)

4 lime leaves

5cm/2in piece of fresh galangal

125ml/4fl oz coconut milk

2 tbsp Thai green curry paste

175ml/6fl oz coconut cream

2 tbsp fish sauce

1 tbsp chopped coriander

Juice of ½ lime

LIME STOCK

2 stalks lemongrass

1cm/½in root ginger

1 clove garlic

½ chilli, deseeded

½ lime

BABY AUBERGINES

8 baby aubergines, halved

50ml/2fl oz olive oil

1 tsp rock salt

Serves 4

Place all the lime stock ingredients in a casserole and simmer for 15 minutes. Bring to the boil and boil until reduced by a quarter. Strain the stock and rinse the casserole.

Season the chicken pieces with salt and pepper. Heat the olive oil in a large casserole dish and brown the chicken over a medium heat. Cover the pan, reduce the heat and cook for 25 minutes, turning the chicken pieces occasionally.

Meanwhile, prepare the baby aubergines. Preheat a chargrill or griddle pan. Rub the aubergines with olive oil and rock salt and grill for about 5 minutes on each side, or until tender.

Place the chicken stock, lime leaves and galangal in a large pan. Bring to the boil, then remove from the heat and leave to infuse for 15 minutes. Strain the stock and return to the pan. Add the lime stock and boil vigorously for about 15 minutes, or until reduced by half.

Stir in the coconut milk, curry paste, fish sauce and cream then add the chicken pieces. Sprinkle with the chopped coriander and lime juice.

Serve with the baby aubergines and sticky rice.

The robust red wine sauce goes well with the firm flesh of the monkfish.

braised monkfish

with haricots, pearl onions and red wine sauce

Preheat the oven to 180°C/350°F/Gas mark 4.

Heat a large casserole dish over moderate heat and add the olive oil and butter. Season the monkfish, add to the dish and cook for about 1 minute on all sides to seal. Remove the fish with a slotted spoon and keep warm.

Add the pearl onions, garlic and thyme and brown for a few minutes. Pour in the red wine and chicken stock. Drain the haricot beans and add to the casserole. Cover and cook in the preheated oven for about 1 hour, or until the beans are tender.

Add the monkfish, cover and return to the oven for a further 10 minutes. Season to taste and serve immediately.

you will need

2 tbsp olive oil	1 bottle of dark red wine
50g/2oz butter	1 litre/1¾ pints Chicken Stock
Salt and freshly ground black pepper	(see page 153)
1kg/2lb monkfish tails, trimmed	250g/9oz haricot beans,
450g/1 lb pearl onions	soaked overnight
4 cloves garlic, crushed	
4 large sprigs thyme	Serves 4

Remember to allow time to soak the lentils overnight, otherwise this dish with its subtle amalgam of flavours is easy to prepare.

smoked chicken

with mixed salad and puy lentils

Mix the olive oil, balsamic vinegar and shallots in a bowl and leave for 2 hours.

Place the lentils, chicken stock, carrot, onion and garlic in a casserole and simmer for 40 minutes. Drain and cool.

Mix half the shallot vinaigrette with the lentils and leave to sit for 30 minutes. Mix the chicken into the lentils. Toss the salad leaves with the remaining vinaigrette and serve with the chicken and lentils.

you will need

150g/¼ pint olive oil

6 tbsp balsamic vinegar

2 shallots, finely diced

100g/3½oz puy lentils, soaked overnight and drained

1 litre/1¾pints Chicken Stock (see page 153)

1 carrot, chopped

½ onion, chopped

½ head of garlic, peeled and crushed

4 breasts of smoked chicken, finely chopped

250g/8oz mixed salad leaves, such as rocket, lollo rosso, oak leaf and mizuna

Serves 4

Paprika, with its mild flavour and striking colour, is an important ingredient in Hungarian cooking, and especially in this traditional meat stew. Make sure your paprika is fresh, and do not be tempted to use chilli powder as a substitute – it is much too hot.

hungarian beef goulash

Preheat the oven to 200°C/400°F/Gas mark 6. Heat the butter in a large, heavy casserole, season the topside and add to the dish. Add the onions and cook for 2 minutes, stirring. Add the paprika and flour, mix well and place in the preheated oven, uncovered, for 10 minutes.

you will need

100g/3½oz butter

1kg/2lb topside, cut into cubes

Salt and freshly ground black pepper

500g/1lb onions, chopped

50g/2oz paprika

50g/2oz flour

1 tbsp tomato purée

2 litres/3½ pints Beef Stock (see page 153)

250g/8oz carrots, cut into chunks

500g/1lb potatoes, peeled and cut into chunks

Chopped parsley, to garnish

Serves 4

Remove from the oven and mix in the tomato purée. Reduce the oven temperature to 180°C/350°/Gas mark 4. Add enough of the stock to cover the meat. Bring to the boil on top of the stove and season. Cover with a lid and return to the oven for 2 hours.

After 1½ hours, mix in the chopped carrots and potatoes and cook for another 30 minutes, or until the meat and vegetables are tender. Sprinkle with chopped parsley to serve.

braised ham hocks

with thyme and rosemary

Rinse the ham hocks and place in a large heavy-based casserole with the carrots, onion, celery, garlic, thyme and water. Bring to the boil on top of the stove, then reduce the heat to very low and simmer for 4 hours.

Strain, reserving the cooking liquid, and discard the vegetables and flavourings. Return the liquid to the casserole and reduce over a high heat to about 600ml/1 pint. Preheat the oven to 150°C/300°F/Gas mark 2.

Return the hocks to the casserole with the braising vegetables and turn to coat with the reduced liquid. Transfer the casserole to the preheated oven and glaze for 45 minutes. Sprinkle the hocks with chopped parsley and serve with mashed potatoes.

you will need

4 ham hocks, soaked for 12 hours in cold water

2 carrots, sliced

1 onion, sliced

2 sticks celery, chopped

½ head garlic

2 sprigs thyme

5 litres/8 pints water

BRAISING VEGETABLES

4 medium carrots

2 small turnips

6 cloves garlic

Chopped parsley, to serve

Serves 4

A new look for an old favourite. Peas and broad beans can be added at the last minute to give a touch of green and a summery feel to this dish.

modern irish stew

with thyme and rosemary

Place the lamb in a heavy casserole with the water and salt and bring to the boil. Skim any fat off the surface and simmer for 30 minutes. Add half the potatoes and simmer for another 30 minutes, stirring to break up the potatoes.

Add the remaining potatoes, the other vegetables, and the thyme and rosemary. Simmer for 30 minutes or until the vegetables and meat are tender.

Stir in the parsley, cream and butter and serve. If using peas and beans stir them in at the last minute.

you will need

1kg/2lb boneless shoulder, neck or shank of lamb, trimmed of fat

1 litre/1¾ pints water

Salt

250g/8oz potatoes, peeled and cut into coarse chunks

250g/8oz carrots, thickly sliced

250g/8oz leeks, thickly sliced

250g/8oz pearl onions

2 sprigs thyme

2 sprigs rosemary

250g/8oz parsley, chopped

250ml/8fl oz double cream

1 tbsp unsalted butter

250g/8oz fresh peas, cooked (optional)

250g/8oz broad beans, cooked (optional)

Serves 4

roasting tin

This is a rectangular, metal, low-sided pan. The sides should be low to allow direct heat to come into contact with a joint of meat, but high enough to contain the juices from the food. The juices can often be used to make a thicker sauce, so the roasting pan should be heavy enough to withstand the heat of the hob or stove.

This is one of those dishes that more or less cooks itself while you get on with something else. The end result is really tasty, perfect for a cold winter's night.

braised lamb shanks

with thyme, roast carrot and pearl onions

you will need

4 lamb shanks, trimmed of excess fat and knuckle removed

2 tbsp olive oil

200g/7oz carrots, cut into chunks

12 pearl onions

3 sprigs thyme

2 tbsp water

Salt and freshly ground black pepper

25g/1oz butter

1 tbsp chopped flat-leaf parsley

1 tbsp chopped thyme

Serves 4

Preheat the oven to 150°C/300°F/Gas mark 3.

Heat the oil in a large roasting tin on top of the stove. Brown the shanks on all sides, then remove from the tin. Add the carrots and onions and cook until golden brown, then remove from the tin.

Return the lamb shanks and any juices to the roasting tin with the thyme and water. Season with salt and pepper, then place in the oven and cook for 2 hours, turning occasionally. Return the carrots and onions to the tin and continue to cook for 1 hour.

Remove from the oven and transfer the lamb shanks and vegetables to warm plates. Remove the thyme sprigs. Skim off the fat from the juices in the roasting tin, then bring to the boil on top of the stove. Reduce for a few minutes until it has the consistency of a light sauce. Remove from the heat, add the butter and season to taste.

Spoon some sauce over each shank and garnish with flat-leaf parsley and thyme.

Squab (baby pigeon) is much more tender than the adult wild pigeon and has a milder flavour. It is also much more expensive. Allow one per person.

roast squab

with green olives, saffron and preserved lemon

you will need

2 tsp hot paprika

2 tsp turmeric

2 tsp ground cumin

125ml/4fl oz olive oil, plus 1 tbsp

6 x 400g/13oz squabs

24 red shallots

25g/1oz ghee or clarified butter

6 cloves garlic, crushed

2 tsp freshly minced root ginger

100g/3½oz squab livers

1.2 litres/2 pints squab stock or Chicken Stock (see page 153)

12 large green olives, pitted and quartered

1 tsp saffron

1 preserved lemon, finely chopped

2tbsp lemon juice

½ teaspoon freshly ground black pepper

40g/1½oz unsalted butter, diced

1 tbsp chopped coriander leaves.

Serves 6

Preheat the oven to 200°C/400°F/Gas mark 6. Mix half the paprika, turmeric and cumin with the olive oil. Brush the squabs inside and out with the spiced olive oil.

Slice 12 shallots. Heat the ghee in a large heavy-based roasting tin over a moderate heat. Add the sliced shallots, garlic, ginger and squab livers and fry for 2 minutes. Add the remaining paprika, turmeric and cumin and cook for another 2 minutes. Pour in the stock and bring to the boil, then reduce the heat and simmer until the stock has reduced by half.

Strain the sauce through a fine sieve, return to the tin and bring to the boil. Add the remaining shallots and simmer for 15 minutes. Add the olives, saffron and preserved lemon and simmer for another 5 minutes, then remove from the heat. Pour the sauce into a bowl and keep warm.

Add the tablespoon of oil to the roasting tin over a high heat. Add the squabs and cook for 2–3 minutes, turning until seared on all sides. Transfer to the preheated oven and roast for 8 minutes. Remove the squabs from the tin and keep warm.

Return the sauce to the tin to warm through. Whisk in the lemon juice, pepper and butter and stir in the coriander leaves. Place a squab in the centre of each plate and pour the sauce around the edge. Serve whole or cut in half.

In Donegal there used to be a famous saying: the potatoes were so good, they ate the skins and all. Years ago, people would have had a heart attack if asked to peel the potatoes before cooking – peeling was done after cooking, if at all.

roast new potatoes

with rock salt and rosemary

Preheat the oven to 180°C/350°F/Gas mark 4. Place the potatoes in a large roasting tin, drizzle with the olive oil and sprinkle with 2 teaspoons of the salt and the pepper. Bake in the preheated oven for about 30 minutes, or until the potatoes are golden brown and starting to shrivel slightly.

you will need

750g/1½lb baby new potatoes

100ml/3½fl oz olive oil

3 tsp rock salt

Freshly ground black pepper

5 sprigs rosemary

2 cloves garlic, crushed

50g/2oz butter

Serves 4

Add the rosemary, garlic and butter. Shake the roasting tin and bake for another 10 minutes. These potatoes can be served hot or warm, sprinkled with the remaining salt.

These confit potatoes could not be simpler to cook, but the taste is out of this world. They are perfect to serve with duck or squab, and are also very good cooked over a barbecue.

confit sweet potatoes

with garlic and thyme

Preheat the oven to 180°C/350°F/Gas mark 4.

you will need

500g/1lb sweet potatoes, cut into 5mm/¼in thick slices

250ml/8fl oz olive oil

Rock salt

Freshly ground black pepper

2 cloves garlic, crushed

2 sprigs thyme

4 tbsp balsamic vinegar

Serves 4

Place the potatoes in a roasting tin, drizzle with half the olive oil and sprinkle very generously with rock salt and black pepper. Bake for 30 minutes, or until tender, shaking the tin occasionally to prevent them sticking.

Five minutes before they are ready, add the garlic and thyme. Shake the potatoes well and cook for another few minutes. Drizzle with the remaining olive oil and the balsamic vinegar. Serve immediately.

chargrill & grill

Chargrilling covers the use of several utensils – griddle pans, grill pans, and even barbecues. The beauty of chargrilling is that the food is cooked quickly and without mess. When the food has been marinated or coated little oil is needed, as chargrilling at high temperatures cooks the food in its own juices. When the food is to be coated in olive oil, make sure it is only a light coating, and that you use a high-quality oil.

Squid is now very trendy, and can be found cooked in all sorts of ways. It makes perfect barbecue food, and has the great advantage that it is easy to cook and can stand up to strong flavours.

chilli salt & pepper squid

with vermicelli

you will need

3 red chillies, deseeded and chopped finely

1 tbsp sea salt flakes

1 tsp freshly ground black pepper

12 baby squid, halved

2 tbsp olive oil

100g/3½oz rice vermicelli

2 tbsp soy sauce

2 tbsp lime juice

3 tbsp coriander leaves

1 tbsp brown sugar

2 tsp fish sauce

Serves 4

Mix the chillies, salt and pepper in a bowl. Brush the squid lightly with oil then dip the pieces into the bowl to coat with the chilli mixture.

Place the rice vermicelli in a bowl and pour on enough boiling water to cover. Leave to soak for 5 minutes, or until tender, then drain. Toss the vermicelli with the soy sauce, lime juice, coriander, sugar and fish sauce. Divide the vermicelli between 2 serving bowls.

To cook the squid, preheat a chargrill or frying pan over a medium heat. Add the squid and cook for 10–15 seconds on each side. Arrange the squid on top of the vermicelli and serve immediately.

Salmon is ideal for grilling or chargrilling, being an oily fish. It goes perfectly with Mediterranean vegetables, with a spoonful of pesto on top. This makes a very good lunch dish, since it is so easy to prepare.

chargrilled salmon

with mediterranean vegetables and pesto

Brush the vegetables and salmon with olive oil and season heavily. Place the potatoes and onions on the chargrill for about 15 minutes, turning occasionally to get a criss-cross effect. Repeat with the peppers, courgettes and aubergines.

Half-way through cooking the vegetables, place the salmon on the grill skin-side down and cook for about 3 minutes on both sides.

Serve the salmon and vegetables with some pesto on each plate.

you will need

8 large new potatoes, boiled and skinned

2 red onions, quartered

2 red peppers, deseeded and quartered

2 yellow peppers, deseeded and quartered

2 courgettes, sliced lengthways

2 aubergines, sliced lengthways

4 x 175g/6oz fillets of wild salmon

3 tbsp olive oil

Salt and freshly ground black pepper

8 tbsp Basil Pesto (see page 155)

Serves 4

Again, an incredibly simple dish, ideal for lunch. Just remember to allow time to marinate the salmon overnight.

ginger-glazed salmon

with mesclun and ginger

Mix all the ingredients for the marinade together in a shallow dish. Add the salmon, turn to coat well and leave to marinate in the fridge overnight.

you will need

4 x 175g/6ox salmon fillets

4 handfuls mesclun

4 tbsp vinaigrette

MARINADE

50ml/2fl oz olive oil

2 tbsp soft brown sugar

10cm/4in root ginger, peeled and grated

2 tbsp sea salt

freshly ground black pepper

Serves 4

Preheat the grill to high. Line the grill pan with foil and oil well. Lay on the salmon and grill on both sides for 1 minute. The salmon will be a little rare in the middle. Simply grill for a few minutes longer if you prefer it well done.

Toss the salad leaves with the vinaigrette and arrange in the centre of each plate. Place the salmon fillets on top and serve immediately.

Oven-dried tomatoes, so easy to prepare, have a rich sweetness that gives added depth to this attractive salad.

octopus with roasted pepper,

olives and sun-dried tomato pesto

Mix the octopus and tentacles in a shallow dish with the olive oil, salt and pepper.

For the tomato dressing, whisk together all the ingredients until well incorporated. Place the peppers, oven-dried tomato, onion, olives and basil in a large bowl. Pour on the tomato dressing and mix well.

Heat a chargrill until very hot and lay on the octopus and tentacles. Using tongs, toss the octopus continuously to ensure even cooking. Add the cooked octopus to the mizuna leaves, mix well and place on 4 plates. Spoon a teaspoon of tomato pesto on top of each and serve with the red pepper salad.

you will need

1kg/2lb baby octopus, tentacles halved

100ml/3½ fl oz olive oil

Salt and freshly ground black pepper

6 tbsp roasted red pepper strips

3 tbsp oven-dried tomatoes, thinly sliced (see page 155)

1 red onion, finely sliced

200g/7oz black olives

2 tbsp basil leaves

2 tbsp shredded mizuna leaves

6 tsp sun-dried tomato pesto

TOMATO DRESSING

1 tbsp sun-dried tomato paste

2 tbsp balsamic vinegar

125ml/4fl oz olive oil

½ tsp salt

½ tsp freshly ground black pepper

Serves 4

You will need a large pan for steaming open the mussels, as well as a grill, but this is still a very quick dish to prepare.

grilled mussels with lemon

and garlic breadcrumbs

you will need

20–30 fresh mussels, scrubbed and rinsed, with

beards removed

4 cloves garlic, crushed

2 shallots, roughly chopped

1 stalk lemongrass

2 tbsp white wine

2 tbsp water

2 tbsp chopped parsley

2 tbsp chopped basil

2 tbsp chopped coriander

Grated zest of 1 lemon

3 tbsp fresh breadcrumbs

90ml/3fl oz olive oil

50g/2oz butter, melted

Salt and freshly ground black pepper

Serves 4

Place the mussels in a large pan with half the garlic, the shallots, lemongrass, wine and water. Cover and steam over a high heat for about 5 minutes, or until the shells have opened. Discard any mussels that do not open.

Remove the empty shell from each mussel and lay the remaining mussels in a large heatproof serving dish. Preheat the grill to high. Mix the remaining garlic with the rest of the ingredients. Spoon this mixture over each mussel and grill until golden and bubbling. Serve immediately with good crusty white bread to mop up all the juices.

you will need

20–30 raw tiger prawns, shelled and deveined

150ml/¼ pint olive oil

4 tsp rock salt

Freshly ground black pepper

500g/1lb dried fettuccine

500/1lb cherry tomatoes, halved

1 clove garlic, crushed

Large bunch of fresh parsley,
roughly chopped

100g/3½oz butter

Serves 4

Fettuccine alfredo was one of the first pasta dishes I ever sampled. Pasta was not very popular in Ireland when I was growing up, but fortunately I had an adventurous mother.

fettuccine

with chargrilled prawns and cherry tomatoes

Place the prawns in a shallow dish with 50ml/2fl oz of the olive oil, 2 teaspoons of rock salt and plenty of black pepper. Leave to marinate for 1 hour.

Preheat the chargrill. Drain the prawns, chargrill for 2–3 minutes on each side, and remove. Brush the tomatoes with olive oil and place briefly on the chargrill to heat through. Remove and sprinkle with the garlic and parsley. Season well.

Cook the pasta in plenty of boiling salted water for about 8 minutes, until al dente. Drain and toss with the remaining olive oil and the butter. Add the tomatoes and prawns, toss well and serve.

This one of my favourite dishes, served at Lloyd's Brasserie. Lorcan tried to take it off the menu once, but the customers complained so much that it has returned to stay.

lorcan gribbons's chicken

with piquillo peppers, guacamole and chilli oil

To make the guacamole, mash the avocado with a fork or in a food processor. Mix in the lemon juice, garlic, chilli, onion and chopped coriander. Season to taste.

Preheat the chargrill or griddle pan and lightly brush the chicken with some chilli oil. Place the chicken strips on the pan and grill for 5 minutes on both sides until the chicken is golden brown.

To serve, spoon some guacamole onto each plate. Top with cos lettuce and arrange some chicken and peppers on top. Spoon some more guacamole onto each plate and drizzle with chilli oil. Serve immediately.

you will need

4 chicken breasts, skinned and
each cut into 5 strips

Chilli oil

2 cos lettuces, large leaves torn in half

1 can Spanish red peppers, drained and halved

1 bunch coriander

GUACAMOLE

3 ripe avocados, peeled and stoned

Juice of ½ lemon

1 clove garlic, crushed

1 medium chilli, deseeded and diced

½ medium red onion, diced

½ bunch of coriander, roughly chopped

Salt and freshly ground black pepper

Serves 4

This was created by chef Gavin and is served at the Metropolitan, Donegal. It incorporates a unique blend of European and Asian flavours.

chargrilled asian chicken

with spiced aioli and bok choy

you will need

4 chicken breasts, skinned and cut into strips

4 heads bok choy, blanched and refreshed

MARINADE

200ml/7fl oz corn oil

2.5cm/1in root ginger, peeled and grated

3 cloves garlic, crushed

100ml/3½fl oz soy sauce

2 tsp curry powder

2 tsp honey

Freshly ground black pepper

SPICED AÏOLI

2 egg yolks

5cm/2in root ginger, peeled and grated

2 cloves garlic, crushed

2 tsp salt

1 tbsp Dijon mustard

3 tbsp lime juice

120-150ml/3-5fl oz sunflower oil

Serves 4

Combine all the ingredients for the aïoli in a food processor, except the oil. Leave the machine running and gradually add the oil in a slow steady stream. Add enough oil until the mixture has thickened, then refrigerate until ready to use.

Mix together the marinade ingredients in a shallow dish. Place the chicken strips in the marinade and turn to coat. Leave for at least 40–50 minutes, longer if possible.

Preheat the chargrill. Lay on the chicken strips and char-grill for 5 minutes on each side, then remove. Add the bok choy and grill for 3–4 minutes, turning to grill evenly.

To serve, arrange chicken and bok choy on each plate and drizzle with aïoli.

Quick and simple, but try to allow time to marinade the lamb overnight – it makes all the difference in the world, giving the meat time to absorb the flavours of the herbs.

kebab of lamb

with mediterranean vegetables in pitta bread

First make the hummus. Place the drained chickpeas in a food processor with the garlic and olive oil and blend until smooth .

Mix the rosemary, thyme and garlic with the olive oil in a shallow dish. Add the lamb, turn to coat well and leave to marinate overnight.

Thread the lamb, aubergine, courgette and pepper on large skewers, alternating meat and vegetables. Grill on a griddle pan or barbecue for about 5 minutes on each side.

Serve with warmed pitta bread and hummus on a bed of beansprouts and mesclun, with a spoonful of curried yogurt.

you will need

1 tablespoon chopped rosemary

1 tablespoon chopped thyme

1 clove garlic, crushed

4 tbsp olive oil

1.25kg/2½lb lamb fillets, trimmed and diced

1 aubergine, diced

1 courgette, diced

1 red pepper, deseeded and diced

1 yellow pepper, deseeded and diced

4 pitta breads

25g/1oz beansprouts

25g/1oz mesclun

Curried yogurt

HUMMUS

1 x 400g/14oz can chickpeas,

rinsed and drained

2 cloves garlic, crushed

50ml/2fl oz olive oil

Serves 4

Figs are one of my favourite fruits. This simple gratin makes the perfect little midnight dessert to finish off dinner after a show.

gratin of figs

with mascarpone

you will need

12 ripe figs

100g/3½oz mascarpone

6 tbsp fructose

3 egg yolks

Juice of 1 lemon

Serves 4

Cut each fig into 5 slices and lay in a grill pan. Mix the mascarpone with 5 tablespoons of the fructose, the egg yolks and lemon juice. Spoon into 4 ramekins and sprinkle with the remaining fructose. Place the figs and ramekins under a preheated grill and cook until the surface of the ramekins is golden brown.

wok

The wok is ideal for one-pot cooking - quick and easy, and almost impossible to get wrong! Once exclusively oriental in style, it is now considered one of the most healthy ways of preparing food. As to flat-bottomed or round, I prefer the round as it allows you to cook meat, fish and vegetables rapidly. The wok can also steam – many woks are supplied with steaming racks for this purpose. They should be seasoned before use, and wiped after use, not washed.

Being a fatty meat, duck is ideal for cooking at high heat in a wok, the initial stir-frying helping to render out a lot of the fat. Cranberries make a colourful addition – use frozen if fresh are unavailable.

stir-fried duck breast

with broad beans, cranberries and shiitake

Heat 1 tablespoon of oil in a wok until smoking. Place the duck breasts skin-side down and cook for 1 minute until the fat starts to render out. Remove the breasts from the wok with a slotted spoon and leave to rest for a few minutes, then slice finely. Wipe the wok clean with kitchen paper.

Heat the other tablespoon of oil in the wok over moderate heat. Add the shallots and sliced duck and stir-fry for 1–2 minutes. Add the shiitake and fresh cranberries. Pour in the chicken stock and simmer until reduced by half. Finally add the cranberry jelly and broad beans. Cook for 1 more minute and sprinkle with chopped tarragon before serving.

you will need

2 tbsp vegetable oil

4 duck breasts

3 shallots, sliced

500g/1lb shiitake mushrooms, sliced

20 fresh cranberries

300m/½ pint Chicken Stock (see page153)

2 tbsp cranberry jelly

650g/1¼lb fresh broad beans, blanched

1 tbsp chopped tarragon leaves

Serves 4

stir-fried bok choy

with shiitake and ginger

you will need

1 tbsp olive oil

500g/1lb bok choy, thinly sliced

)0ml/3½ fl oz Chicken Stock (see page 153)

2 tbsp oyster sauce

2 tbsp soy sauce

2 cloves garlic, crushed

100g/3½ oz shiitake mushrooms

5cm/1in root ginger, peeled and grated

6 spring onions, roughly chopped

1 tbsp sesame oil

1 tsp sugar

Salt and freshly ground black pepper

Serves 4

Heat the olive oil in a wok and stir-fry the bok choy until just starting to soften. Add the stock, oyster sauce and soy sauce. Stir and add the garlic, mushrooms and ginger. Stir-fry over a high heat for 2–3 minutes and then add the remaining ingredients.
Season well and serve.

scallop & shiitake

stir-fry

Heat both the oils in a wok and add the scallops. Toss for a minute then add the shiitake mushrooms, bok choy stems and sugar-snap peas. Stir-fry for 30 seconds.

Add the ginger, garlic and bok choy leaves. Add 1–2 tablespoons of water and stir-fry all together for a minute. Add the lime juice and season to taste.

Serve immediately.

you will need

2 tbsp olive oil

3 tbsp groundnut oil

12 scallops, halved

200g/7oz shiitake mushrooms

2 heads baby bok choi, sliced

40 sugar-snap peas, cut in half

2.5cm/1in root ginger, peeled and chopped

2 cloves garlic, crushed

Juice of 1 lime

Salt and freshly ground black pepper

Serves 4

This elegant confection is delicious, and simple to make, but it does need forward planning as you have to marinate the squid overnight.

soba noodles with soy,

coriander and marinated squid

you will need

150ml/¼ pint olive oil

15g/½oz butter

2 limes, sliced

1 stalk lemongrass, chopped

½ bunch of coriander, chopped

50g/2oz chopped root ginger

500g/1lb baby squid, sliced in rings

150g/5oz soba noodles

3 tbsp soy sauce

2 tbsp chopped coriander

coriander leaves, to garnish

Serves 4

Heat the olive oil and butter in a wok over gentle heat. Add the limes, lemongrass, coriander and ginger and cook for 4 minutes. Remove from the heat and stir in the squid. Transfer to a shallow dish and leave to marinate overnight.

Remove the squid from the marinade with a slotted spoon. Heat 2–3 tablespoons of the marinade in a wok, add the squid and stir-fry for 3–4 minutes.

Put the soba noodles in a large bowl and pour on enough boiling water to cover. Leave for 30 seconds, then drain and add to the squid. Mix well and add the soy sauce and coriander. Serve immediately, garnished with coriander leaves.

The hot, spicy sauce adds a punch to these succulent spring rolls. Everything can be done in the wok, including making the sauce and deep-frying the spring rolls.

crispy spring rolls with duck

and barbecue sauce

To make the barbecue sauce, heat the olive oil in a wok and add all the dry ingredients. Cover and sweat over medium heat for 5 minutes. Add the honey, red wine vinegar, balsamic vinegar and chicken stock. Bring to the boil and boil until reduced by half, then remove from the heat and transfer to a jug. Keep warm. Wipe the wok clean with kitchen paper.

Stir-fry the duck breast in the dry wok over high heat. When the fat starts to render remove the duck from the wok with a slotted spoon and set aside. Wipe the wok clean with kitchen paper.

Heat the sesame oil in the wok and add the peppers, carrot, chilli, ginger, garlic and soy sauce. Stir-fry over a high heat for 2–3 minutes, then add the remaining ingredients and the duck. Transfer the filling to a bowl and wipe the wok clean with kitchen paper.

Brush the spring roll wrappers with the beaten egg. Spoon some of the stir-fried mixture into the centre of each one and roll up, tucking in the ends. Heat the oil in the wok to 180°C/350°F and deep-fry the spring rolls until golden brown. Remove with a slotted spoon and drain on kitchen paper. Serve with the barbecue sauce.

you will need

4 spring roll wrappers

1 egg, beaten

Vegetable oil for deep-frying

FILLING

2 duck breasts, thinly sliced

3 tbsp sesame oil

250g/8oz mixed peppers, deseeded and sliced

1 carrot, sliced

2 chillies, deseeded and diced

2.5cm/1in root ginger, peeled and sliced

1 clove garlic, chopped

1 tbsp soy sauce

75g/3oz sugar snap peas, sliced

175g/6oz beansprouts

25g/1oz sesame seeds

Zest and juice of 1 lemon, lime and orange

BARBECUE SAUCE

2 tbsp olive oil

200g/7oz mixed peppers, deseeded and diced

25g/1oz sesame seeds

25g/1oz cayenne

1 chilli, deseeded and diced

4 shallots, diced

100g/3½oz honey

2 tbsp red wine vinegar

2 tsp balsamic vinegar

275ml/9fl oz Chicken Stock (see page153)

Serves 4

Another dish that is so simply done. Crab claws can be bought separately and only require a very light cooking.

stir-fried crab claws

with spring onion, chilli and garlic

Blend the chilli, garlic and ginger in a food processor until it forms a rough paste. Add the rice vinegar, sugar and salt and mix well.

Heat the vegetable oil in a wok over a medium heat. Add the chilli paste and stir-fry for 1–2 minutes. Add the ginger and crab claws. Stir in the fish sauce and add the spring onions. Toss well, reduce the heat and place a lid or a piece of foil on top. Cook for 2–3 minutes, shaking the wok. Season with black pepper and serve immediately, garnished with spring onion strips and coriander leaves.

you will need

1 red chilli, deseeded and finely chopped

2 cloves garlic, chopped

1cm/½in root ginger, peeled and chopped

1½ tbsp rice wine vinegar

1 tbsp caster sugar

½ teaspoon sea salt

125ml/4fl oz vegetable oil

1 tbsp chilli paste

50g/2oz root ginger, peeled and sliced

4 crab claws, boiled, shell cracked and cleaned

2 tbsp fish sauce (nam pla)

4 spring onions, thinly sliced, green parts reserved for garnish

Freshly ground black pepper

coriander leaves, to garnish

Serves 2

This recipe enables you to get away from the traditional pork with apple sauce. It has a great Thai flavour, the pork curry blending well with the sweetness of the apples.

pork with cider apples

in a yellow curry with fava beans

you will need

4 tbsp vegetable oil

1kg/2lb pork fillets, finely sliced into strips

3 shallots, sliced

1 stalk lemongrass, sliced

2 yellow peppers, deseeded and finely sliced

1 tbsp turmeric

1 tbsp curry powder

2 Granny Smith apples, quartered and cored

300ml/½ pint cider

600ml/1 pint Chicken Stock (see page 153)

900g/1lb 13oz fava (broad) beans, blanched until tender

1 tbsp chopped coriander

Salt and freshly ground black pepper

Serves 4

Heat half the vegetable oil in a preheated wok over high heat. Add the pork strips and sauté until golden brown in colour. Remove the pork from the wok and keep warm.

Wipe out the wok with kitchen paper, then reheat with the remaining oil. Add the shallots, lemongrass and peppers and sauté for 1 minute. Stir in the turmeric and curry power and cook for 1 minute. Add the apples and cook for 2–3 minutes.

Add the cider to the wok and simmer until reduced by half. Add the chicken stock and again simmer until reduced by half. Stir in the fava beans, pork and chopped coriander and season to taste. Serve immediately.

Hot chilli jam adds an explosive note to this delicately flavoured dish.

stir-fried chicken fillets

with shiitake, sweet potato and chilli jam

Heat the oil in a wok on a high heat. Add the chicken and sweet potatoes and stir-fry for 2–3 minutes. Season with salt and pepper and add the coriander.

Add the shiitake mushrooms and stir-fry for 2–3 minutes. Pour in the chicken stock and simmer for 2 minutes, then add the coconut milk and bring to the boil.

Remove from the heat and serve in bowls, garnished with chopped coriander and served with chilli jam.

you will need

2 tbsp olive oil

4 fillets of chicken breast, skinned
and finely sliced

680g/1lb 6oz sweet potatoes,
peeled and grated

Salt and freshly ground black pepper

2 tbsp chopped coriander

500g/1lb shiitake mushrooms, sliced

150ml/¼ pint Chicken Stock (see page 153)

3 tbsp coconut milk

Chopped coriander leaves, to garnish

Chilli Jam (see page 155), to serve

Serves 4

baking sheet

In the restaurant trade we refer to baking sheets as 'flats'. The low sides mean that food can be easily turned, so the cooking time is greatly reduced. The sheets should be made of aluminium and steel, so that they do not warp at high temperatures, and so that they can withstand direct heat if the baking sheet has to be placed on the hob to finish off a dish, or to sear meat.

This colourful salad, served with Parmesan shavings and garlicky baguette croûtons on top, makes an ideal starter.

baby spinach salad

with pancetta, soft-boiled quail's eggs and croûtons

you will need

1 large baguette, sliced

2 cloves garlic, crushed

50ml/2fl oz olive oil

Salt and freshly ground black pepper

100g/3½oz baby spinach

4 tbsp balsamic vinegar

8 slices pancetta

4 soft-boiled quail's eggs, peeled

25g/1oz sun-dried tomato

25g/1oz Parmesan, shaved

Serves 4

Preheat the oven to 180°C/350°F/Gas mark 4. Rub the baguette slices with garlic and place on a baking sheet. Drizzle with the olive oil and season, then bake in the preheated oven for 10 minutes. Place the pancetta on a baking sheet and bake for 1 minute in the oven until crisp.

To serve, toss the spinach with the balsamic vinegar and arrange on a serving dish. Place the baguette slices on top of the spinach. Arrange the eggs, pancetta, sun-dried tomato and Parmesan shavings on top of the spinach.

Baked beetroot is a revelation – sweet and meltingly tender. It makes the perfect foil to slices of toasted goat's cheese, coated in walnut-flavoured breadcrumbs.

baked beetroot,

goat's cheese with walnuts and rocket

Preheat the oven to 160°C/325°F/Gas mark 3. Wrap each bulb of beetroot in foil and bake in the oven for 1 hour, or until tender. Unwrap and allow to cool. Leave the oven at the same temperature.

Peel the beetroot, then cut into even slices and place in a shallow dish. Add half the vinaigrette, turn to coat and leave to marinate.

Peel any rind off the goat's cheese and slice into thick rounds. Brush the cheese with walnut oil and coat each round with the breadcrumbs. Place the rounds on a baking sheet and bake in the oven for 10 minutes to warm the cheese.

Toss the rocket leaves with 1 tablespoon of the vinaigrette. Arrange the leaves in the centre of each plate and place some toasted goat's cheese on top. Arrange some beetroot around the plate. Sprinkle with roasted walnuts and drizzle with the remaining vinaigrette.

you will need

500g/1lb baby beetroot, trimmed

4 tbsp Walnut Vinaigrette (see page 155)

500g/1lb goat's cheese

1 tbsp walnut oil

150g/5oz herbed breadcrumbs

8 rocket leaves

125g/4oz walnuts, oven-roasted

Serves 4

This is ideal for a quick lunch or supper, but it would also make a very elegant starter, provided the main course is not too heavy.

twice-baked potatoes
with crabmeat and walnuts

Preheat the oven to 180°C/350°F/Gas mark 3. Rinse the potatoes under cold water, wrap in foil and bake in the preheated oven for 1 hour. Remove from the oven and allow to cool completely. Leave the oven at the same temperature.

Cut off the top of each potato, leaving two-thirds for the base. Scoop out the inside into a bowl, leaving a 5mm/¼in layer of potato attached to the skin. Add the crème fraîche, herbs, crabmeat and rocket and mix well with the potato. Season to taste with salt and pepper.

Fill each potato with some of the potato mixture. Place on a baking sheet and bake in the preheated oven for 20 minutes, or until golden brown on top. Garnish with fresh herbs and serve on a bed of chopped walnuts and chives.

you will need

4 baking potatoes, about 150g/5oz each

100ml/3½fl oz crème fraîche

2 tbsp chopped chives, parsley, or other fresh herbs

100g/3½oz crabmeat

Salt and freshly ground black pepper

Fresh herb leaves, to garnish

Chopped walnuts and chives, to serve

Serves 4

This is one of the healthiest ways to cook fish, and also has the advantage of being one of the easiest – it is almost impossible to burn or overcook anything this way.

salmon and leeks

en papillotte

you will need

100g/3½oz butter

4 x 175g/6oz salmon fillets

2 leeks, finely sliced

50ml/2fl oz white wine

50ml/2fl oz olive oil

Salt and freshly ground black pepper

2 tbsp finely chopped chervil

1 tbsp lemon juice

Serves 4

Preheat the oven to 180°C/350°F/Gas mark 4.

Smear 4 large circles of nonstick baking paper with the butter. Place a salmon fillet in the centre of each one and top with a quarter of the leeks. Pour a quarter of the white wine and olive oil over each fillet and season well. Add the chervil, then draw up the edges of the paper to seal the parcels.

Place the parcels on a baking sheet and cook in the oven for about 10–15 minutes, depending on how well done you like the salmon. Carefully unwrap the parcels so that you do not get burned from the steam and try to keep as much of the juice as possible. Place each fillet on a plate and spoon some of the leek mixture on top. Serve immediately, sprinkled with lemon juice.

There are many variations of this delicious galette that you can try, such as using sliced courgettes insead of tomatoes, and rocket instead of mixed herbs – whatever takes your fancy.

baked tomato

and tapenade galette

Warm the goat's cheese and cream in a small pan and mix until well combined. Remove from the heat and add pepper and the chopped basil. Set aside.

you will need

4 x 15cm/6in rounds of puff pastry,
1cm/½in thick

4 tablespoons Sun-dried Tomato
Tapenade (see page 155)

8 medium plum tomatoes

4 tablespoons Tomato Oil
(see page 152)

Salt and freshly ground
black pepper

Selection of chopped fresh herbs,
such as chives, parsley, chervil, basil

4 tablespoons balsamic vinegar

GOAT'S CHEESE MIXTURE

300g/10oz goat's cheese, chopped

100ml/3½ fl oz double cream

Freshly ground black pepper

2 tablespoons chopped basil

Serves 4

Preheat the oven to 180°C/350°F/Gas mark 4. Place the puff pastry rounds between 2 sheets of greaseproof paper and place on a baking sheet. Lay another baking sheet on top (to ensure that the pastry won't rise), and bake for 15 minutes. Remove from the oven and leave to cool on a wire rack. Turn down the oven to a low temperature.

Spread the pastry rounds with the sundried tomato tapenade. Spoon a small amount of the goat's cheese mixture into the centre of each round. Slice the plum tomatoes thinly and arrange on top. Drizzle the rounds with tomato oil, season with salt and pepper and put in a low oven to warm for 3–4 minutes.

Serve sprinkled with fresh herbs, drizzled with balsamic vinegar.

The tangy cheese perfectly balances the richness of the ham in these exciting parcels, served on a bed of mixed salad leaves.

baked goat's cheese

with prosciutto

you will need

400g/13oz hard goat's cheese

4 large slices prosciutto

4 basil leaves

Freshly ground black pepper

2 tbsp olive oil

Mixed salad , to serve

Serves 4

Preheat the oven to 200°C/400°F/Gas mark 6.

Remove the rind from the goat's cheese and cut into 4 slices.
Lay out the prosciutto and place a basil leaf in the centre of each piece. Place a slice of goat's cheese on top and season with black pepper. Wrap up neatly in the prosciutto, then tightly wrap with clingfilm. Chill for about 1 hour.

Remove the clingfilm from the parcels and place on a baking sheet. Drizzle with olive oil and bake in the preheated oven for 10 minutes. The prosciutto should just start to crisp.

Serve with a mixed salad.

This pizza is simple enough to prepare, the oven-dried tomatoes adding a delicious sweetness to the topping.

white cheese pizza

with artichoke, rocket and oven-dried tomatoes

To make the dough, mix all the dry ingredients in a food processor. Mix the water and yeast and gradually add to the flour on a medium speed for 10 minutes, until a smooth dough is formed.

Shape the pizza dough into 4 very thin discs on a greased baking sheet and leave to rest for 30 minutes. Preheat the oven to 180°C/350°F/Gas mark 4. Place the garlic on a baking sheet, sprinkle with the olive oil and roast for 10 minutes. Remove the garlic from the skins.

you will need

6 cloves garlic

1 tbsp olive oil

1 recipe Oven-dried Tomatoes (see page 155)

250g/8oz rocket

1 can artichoke hearts, drained

900g/1lb 13oz buffalo mozzarella, sliced

PIZZA DOUGH

500g/1lb plain flour

1 tsp salt

Pinch of sugar

500ml/16fl oz warm water

10g/½oz fresh yeast

Serves 4

Bake the pizza bases in the preheated oven for 20 minutes. Remove from the oven and reduce the temperature to 160°C/325°F/Gas mark 3.

Spread the dried tomatoes over the bases and cover with rocket. Arrange the artichokes on top and sprinkle with the unpeeled roast garlic. Place slices of mozzarella on top and sprinkle with olive oil. Return the pizzas to the oven for 20 minutes.

You can make lots of variations on this theme, using shrimps, scallops or artichokes instead of the chorizo, for example, and mozzarella or blue cheese in place of the goat's cheese.

tomato & goat's cheese pizza

with chorizo and rocket

you will need

900g/1lb 13oz plain Pizza Dough (see page 123)

6 ripe plum tomatoes, sliced

1 x 125g/4oz log of goat's cheese, sliced, plus extra for sprinkling

20 thin slices of chorizo (about 125g/4oz)

Rock salt and freshly ground black pepper

500g/1lb rocket

50ml/2fl oz olive oil

Serves 4

Shape the pizza dough into 4 very thin discs on a greased baking sheet. Leave to rest for 30 minutes. Preheat the oven to 180°C/350°F/Gas mark 4.

Bake the pizza bases for 20 minutes in the preheated oven, then remove from the heat and allow to cool. Reduce the oven temperature to 160°C/325°F/Gas mark 3.

Cover the bases with alternate layers of tomatoes, goat's cheese and chorizo. Season with rock salt and black pepper and bake in the preheated oven until the cheese has melted, about 10 minutes.

Toss the rocket with the olive oil and season. Serve the pizza with the rocket piled on top.

I love eating chocolate with coffee, and these cookies and muffins make perfect petit fours. Both are simple to make and store perfectly.

chunky chocolate cookies

Preheat the oven to 190°C/375°F/Gas mark 5. Lightly grease 2 baking sheets.

you will need

50g/2oz lightly salted butter, plus extra for greasing

150g/5oz plain flour

½ tsp bicarbonate of soda

75g/3oz caster sugar

1 egg, beaten

175g/6oz plain or milk chocolate, chopped into small pieces

100g/3½ oz white chocolate, chopped into small pieces

Demerara sugar

Serves 20

Melt the butter in a small pan, then allow to cool slightly. Sift the flour and bicarbonate of soda into a bowl. Add the sugar, melted butter, vanilla and egg. Stir in the chocolate. Using a dessertspoon, place spoonfuls of the mixture on the baking sheets, spacing them well apart, and sprinkle with the sugar.

Bake the cookies for about 15 minutes until golden around the edges. Remove from the oven and leave on the baking sheet for 5 minutes, then transfer to a wire rack to cool.

mini chocolate muffins

Preheat the oven to 160°C/325°F/Gas mark 3.

Place the egg, butter and vanilla in a bowl and beat well together. Sieve the flour, salt and baking powder into the bowl. Stir in the muscovado sugar, then add the milk and lightly fold in with a metal spoon. Do not over-mix. Stir in the chocolate.

Spoon the mixture into a buttered mini muffin sheet. Sprinkle with demerara sugar and bake for 10 minutes until risen. Cool on a wire rack.

you will need

1 egg, beaten

30g/1½oz melted butter,
plus extra for greasing

Few drops of vanilla essence

80g/3½oz self-raising flour

Pinch of salt

½ tsp baking powder

30g/1½oz light muscovado sugar

50ml/2fl oz milk

50g/2oz white chocolate, chopped

2 tbsp demerara sugar

Serves 20

You could also flavour the bread with other herbs, such as thyme or rosemary. Bread recipes usually tell you to leave the dough to rise in a warm place, but in fact it is best to let it rise slowly at room temperature.

sun-dried tomato

and basil bread

In a food processor, mix together the flour and salt. Cream the yeast with the sugar and 1–2 tablespoons of the warm water. Mix the remaining water with the tomato purée and add to the flour with the yeast mixture, sun-dried tomatoes, basil and olive oil. Process until the dough comes together and feel quite soft but not sticky. Add more water if necessary.

you will need

750g/1½lb plain flour

1 tsp salt

15g/½oz fresh yeast or 1 tbsp fast-acting dried yeast

1 tsp sugar

300ml/½ pint warm water

4 tbsp tomato purée

200g/7oz sun-dried tomatoes in olive oil,
drained and finely chopped

1 tbsp finely chopped basil

4 tbsp olive oil

Makes 1 large loaf

Turn the dough out onto a lightly floured surface and knead until smooth and elastic, about 10 minutes. Place the dough in a lightly greased bowl, cover with a tea towel and leave to rise at room temperature for 1 ½–2 hours, until doubled in size.

Knock back the dough and shape into a long baguette. Place the dough on a baking sheet, cover with a damp tea towel and leave to prove for 1 ½–2 hours until doubled in size. Preheat the oven to 200°C/400°F/Gas mark 6.

Dust the loaf with flour and sprinkle with a little water. Bake in the preheated oven for 15 minutes, then reduce the temperature to 180°C/350°F/Gas mark 4. Bake for another 25 minutes, or until the loaf sounds hollow when tapped on the bottom. Remove from the baking sheet and leave to cool on a wire rack.

Make the sorbet in advance and store in the freezer.

mango sorbet

with tuiles

Heat the water and sugar in a small pan over gentle heat until the sugar has dissolved. Once the sugar has dissolved, bring to the boil, then simmer for 5 minutes. Allow to cool slightly, then stir into the mango purée and mix well. Pour into a freezer container and freeze until ready to use.

Preheat the oven to 180°C/350°F/Gas mark 4. Line a baking sheet with nonstick baking parchment.

To make the tuiles, whip the butter and sugar until light and creamy then fold in the flour, being careful not to over-mix. Place spoonfuls of the batter on the baking sheet, then spread it out as thinly as possible with the back of a spoon.

Bake in the preheated oven for 10 minutes, then remove with a spatula while still hot and shape by moulding each one round a champagne or other bottle. Leave in position to cool, then fill with sorbet when cold.

you will need

150ml/¼ pint water

30g/1oz sugar

300g/10oz puréed mango, strained

TUILES

300g/10oz butter

300g/10oz sugar

200g/7oz self-raising flour

Serves 4

This is ideal for a quick lunch or supper, but it would also make a very elegant starter, provided the main course is not too heavy.

lemon tart

Preheat the oven to 160°C/325°F/Gas mark 3.

To make the pastry, combine the butter, sugar and flour together in a food processor. Add the eggs and mix to make a smooth dough. Wrap the dough in clingfilm and chill for at least 30 minutes before using.

Roll out the pastry and use to line one 10cm/8in greased flan dish, or 4 individual flan tins. Transfer to the freezer for 20 minutes. Bake straight from the freezer for 10 minutes, or until golden brown. Remove from the oven and leave to cool. Reduce the oven temperature to 100°C/225°F/Gas mark ¼.

To make the filling, bring the cream and lemon zest to the boil in a pan. Combine the sugar, egg yolks and lemon juice in a bowl. Whisk the cream mixture into the egg mixture, combining thoroughly. Strain the filling into the tart shell and bake for 20–30 minutes.

you will need

450g/15oz butter

240g/8oz sugar

700g/1¼lb self-raising flour

2 eggs

FILLING

1 litre/1¾ pints double cream

Zest and juice of 7 lemons

200g/7oz sugar

10 egg yolks

Serves 4

baking dish

The most useful baking dishes are heatproof, so that cooking can be started off on top of the stove, if need be. Dishes come in all shapes and sizes, from the large, oval or rectangular kind used to cook baked pasta, apple crumble and similar dishes, to the small individual ramekins or soufflé dishes used for elegant desserts such as crème brûlée

Squid baked in a Provençal-style sauce is tender and full of flavour.

provençal-style baked squid

with rice pilaf

you will need

4 medium squid tubes

50g/2oz ground almonds

STUFFING

4 tbsp olive oil

1 onion, chopped

4 cloves garlic, finely chopped

150g/5oz short-grain Italian brown rice

300ml/½ pint water

1 bunch of parsley, chopped

4 sprigs oregano, chopped

Salt and freshly ground pepper

TOMATO AND PEPPER SAUCE

100ml/3½ fl oz olive oil

1 onion, sliced

2 cloves garlic, sliced

2 courgettes, sliced

2 red peppers, deseeded and sliced

1 x 400g/14 oz can of tomatoes

1 bay leaf

3 sprigs thyme

200ml/7fl oz water

Salt and freshly ground black pepper

Serves 4

Preheat the oven to 200°C/400°F/Gas mark 6.

To make the sauce, heat the olive oil in a fireproof baking dish over moderate heat, add the onion and garlic, cover and sweat for 3 minutes. Add the courgettes and peppers and sweat for another 3 minutes. Add the tomatoes and their juices, the herbs and water. Bring to the boil and simmer gently for 5 minutes. Season with salt and pepper and remove from the heat. Transfer the sauce to a bowl and rinse out the dish.

To cook the stuffing, heat the olive oil in the dish over moderate heat, add the onion and garlic, cover and sweat for 3 minutes. Add the rice, cover and sweat again for 2 minutes. Pour in the water and cook over a moderate heat for 30 minutes, or until the rice has absorbed all the water.

Mix half the parsley with the rice, add the oregano and season. Stuff the rice mixture into the squid tubes and close the ends with skewers. Pour the tomato sauce into the baking dish and place the stuffed squid on top. Sprinkle with the ground almonds and remaining parsley and bake in the preheated oven for 15–20 minutes. Serve the squid with the sauce spooned on top.

The meaty flesh of monkfish, spiked with garlic, also goes well with the fruity flavours of the Provençal-style sauce.

gigot of monkfish

Preheat the oven to 180°C/350°F/Gas mark 4.

Make 3 incisions with a sharp knife across the back of each piece of monkfish. Insert half a garlic clove into each incision.

Make the sauce in a fireproof baking dish. Place the monkfish on top of the sauce and pour the olive oil over the monkfish. Transfer to the preheated oven and cook for 15 minutes.

To serve, spoon some sauce on each plate and place a piece of monkfish in the centre.

you will need

4 X 200g/7oz monkfish tails

6 cloves garlic, halved

50ml/2fl oz olive oil

Tomato and Pepper Sauce (see page 135)

Baked aubergine has a wonderful smoky flavour and a softly melting texture.

marinated aubergine salad

with baked chicken

Preheat the oven to 180°C/350°F/Gas mark 4. Place the aubergines in a large heat-proof baking dish. Pour the olive oil over them and sprinkle with the garlic, balsamic vinegar and thyme. Season well and cook for 30–40 minutes until tender, turning the aubergines half-way through cooking. Remove from the oven, transfer to a serving dish and keep warm. Increase the temperature to 200°C/400°F/Gas mark 6.

Heat the sunflower oil in the baking dish. Season the chicken breasts and add to the dish. Sear on both sides, then add the butter. Transfer the dish to the oven to finish cooking, about 7–10 minutes.

Reheat the aubergines if necessary and serve with the chicken breasts.

you will need

6 aubergines, cut into large dice

150ml/¼ pint olive oil

2 cloves garlic, crushed

50ml/2fl oz balsamic vinegar

1 tsp chopped thyme

Salt and freshly ground black pepper

2 tbsp sunflower oil

4 chicken breasts

50g/2oz butter

Serves 4

you will need

4–6 plums

4 tablespoons puréed

passion fruit

½ teaspoon star anise

½ teaspoon ground cinnamon

30g/1½oz butter, diced

2 tbsp sugar

CRÈME CHANTILLY

300ml/½ pint double cream

1 vanilla bean, split and seeds removed

25g/1oz icing sugar

Serves 4

This is so simple, and cooks in a few minutes, yet it looks and tastes heavenly. What more could you want?

baked spiced plums

with herbs and crème chantilly

Preheat the oven to 190°C/375°F/Gas mark 5.

Cut the plums in half and remove the stones. Place the plums skin-side down in an ovenproof dish and drizzle with the passion fruit purée. Sprinkle the spices, butter and sugar on top and bake in the preheated oven for 10 minutes.

Remove from the oven and baste with the cooking juices. Lightly whip the cream and fold in the vanilla seeds and icing sugar. Serve the crumble with a spoonful of the crème chantilly on top.

The brûlée is topped with a layer of crisp caramel, with creamy custard and raspberries hiddden underneath.

raspberry & mascarpone

with a layer of crisp caramel

you will need

3 egg yolks

2 eggs

50g/2oz sugar

275ml/9fl oz milk

275ml/9fl oz double cream

2 vanilla pods, split

75g/3oz mascarpone

200g/7oz raspberries, plus a few extra
for decoration

125g/4oz caster sugar

Serves 4

Preheat the oven to 120°C/250°F/Gas mark ½

Whisk the egg yolks and eggs in a bowl with the sugar until pale and creamy. Heat the milk and cream over gentle heat and slowly pour into the egg mixture. Strain through a fine sieve and then scrape in the vanilla seeds. While the mixture is still warm, add the mascarpone and mix well.

Place the raspberries in the bottom of 4 ramekins and pour in the custard. Place the ramekins in a baking dish and half-fill with water. Place in the oven and cook for 30–40 minutes. Remove from the heat and allow to cool.

To finish, sprinkle each ramekin with a layer of caster sugar and glaze under a grill until the sugar melt and caramelises. Allow to cool, then decorate with a few fresh raspberries.

The sweet-sour lime sauce, with its hint of acidity, is the perfect complement to this heavenly sweet mango soufflé.

mango soufflé

with lime sabayon

you will need

4–6 mangoes, peeled and diced

50ml/2fl oz water

Juice and zest of 3 limes

5 egg whites

50g/2oz caster sugar, plus extra for dusting

butter for greasing

LIME SAUCE

3 limes

3 tbsp light brown sugar

25g/1oz unsalted butter

200ml/7fl oz double cream

Serves 4

Place the mangoes in a pan with the water over gentle heat. Simmer for 5 minutes. Add the lime juice and zest. Puree in a food processor and set aside.

Preheat the oven to 180°C/350°F/Gas mark 4.

Beat the egg whites in a large bowl and gently add the caster sugar. With a metal spoon fold the mango puree into the egg mixture. Butter 4 medium-sized soufflé dishes and dust with caster sugar, making sure the dishes are completely coated. Gently pour in the mango mixture and lightly smooth the top. Cook the soufflés for 25 minutes, or until the top has browned and risen.

For the sauce, grate the rind of 2 limes. Mix the zest with the juice of all 3 limes and pour into a small pan. Add the brown sugar and cook over a low heat until the sugar has dissolved. Add the butter and allow to melt, then pour in the cream and stir thoroughly. Bring the sauce to the boil, and let it bubble for 2 minutes until the cream has thickened. Pour the sauce into a jug.

Serve the soufflés immediately they are ready, with the sauce.

Crumble is one of my all-time favourite puddings. Served with cream or ice cream it makes heavenly winter fare.

raisin, pear & apple crumble

you will need

2 Granny Smith apples, peeled, cored and finely diced

2 pears, peeled, cored and finely diced

50/2oz raisins

2 tbsp Cointreau

3 tbsp caster sugar

Pinch of ground cinnamon

200g/7oz flour

100g/3½oz butter, cut into cubes and chilled

50g/2oz demerara sugar

Double cream or ice cream, to serve

Serves 4

Preheat the oven to 180°C/350°F/Gas mark 4.

Mix together the apples, pears, raisins, Cointreau, caster sugar and cinnamon in a bowl. Chill until ready to use.

Sift the flour into a bowl and rub in the butter until the mixture resembles breadcrumbs. Mix in the demerara sugar. Fill 4 individual ramekins or 1 large one with the fruit mixture and top with the pastry. Bake for about 30 minutes, until the fruit is soft and the pastry topping is starting to colour.

Serve with fresh cream or ice-cream.

deep fryer

Abused by images of a smoking chip pan and the smell of stale oil, the deep fryer needs some serious PR. The traditional deep fryer is made of stainless steel, with handles on either side. A basket with long handles allows you to lower food into the fat for rapid cooking at high temperatures. Deep fryers bring out the best in savoury pastries – the goat's cheese wontons are cooked to perfection, the cheese molten, the pastry crisp, and not a chip in sight.

Crisp deep-fried wontons enhance this elegant, piquantly flavoured salad.

spicy asian salad

with goat's cheese wontons

Mix the cabbage, carrot, pepper and ginger in a bowl.

In another bowl mix the soy sauce, peanut butter, sugar, lime juice and chilli. Add to the cabbage mixture, mix well and leave to marinate for 3 hours.

you will need

250g/8oz white cabbage, shredded finely

1 small carrot, cut into long fine strips

1 red pepper, deseeded and cut into long fine strips

2 tbsp dried ginger

4 tbsp soy sauce

1 tbsp peanut butter

1 tbsp sugar

2 tbsp lime juice

½ tablespoon chopped and deseeded chilli

1 packet wonton skins

125g/4oz goat's cheese, crumbled

Vegetable oil for deep-frying

4 tbsp coriander leaves

Serves 4

Drain the salad and mix the goat's cheese with the liquid. Place a teaspoon of the mixture on each wonton skin, wet the edges and gather together to make little parcels.

Heat the oil for deep-frying to 180°C/350°F in a large pan or deep-fryer. Add the wontons and deep-fry for 2–3 minutes, until golden brown.

Serve the wontons with the salad and garnish with coriander leaves .

Ideal party or buffet fare, or for dinner guests to dip into while you get on with the serious cooking. It can all be prepared ahead of time.

mini crabcakes

with dips and asian slaw

Flake the crabmeat into a bowl. Mix with the remaining ingredients and season well. Roll the mixture into small balls, about 1cm/1/2in in diameter, and chill for 2–3 hours.

Heat the oil in a deep-fryer to 180°C/350°F. Deep-fry the cakes until golden brown, then remove with a slotted spoon. Drain on kitchen paper and sprinkle with salt.

Mix all the dips in separate dishes or bowls. Place the slaw ingredients in a salad bowl. Mix together the dressing ingredients and pour over the salad. Toss well. Serve the crabcakes with the dips and salad.

you will need

350g/12oz white crabmeat

2 tbsp finely chopped coriander

1 tbsp finely chopped parsley

Zest and juice of 2 lemons

30ml/1fl oz double cream

2 egg yolks

70g/2½ oz fresh white breadcrumbs

Salt and freshly ground black pepper

Vegetable oil, for deep-frying

DRESSING

150ml/¼ pint olive oil

50ml/2fl oz sesame oil

50ml/2fl oz soy sauce

50ml/2fl oz rice vinegar

2 tbsp sugar

Juice of 1 lime

Salt and freshly ground black pepper

SESAME DIP

50ml/2fl oz sesame oil

50ml/2fl oz peanut oil

3 tbsp honey

2 tbsp soy sauce

3 tbsp hoisin sauce

ASIAN SLAW

2 heads bok choy, sliced and blanched

1 small radiccio lettuce, finely sliced

½ head iceberg lettuce, very finely sliced

3 papaya, peeled and roughly chopped

2 tsp roasted sesame seeds

BARBECUE DIP

3 tbsp ketchup

3 tbsp barbecue sauce

1 tbsp honey

3 tbsp soy sauce

1 tbsp Worcestershire sauce

2 tbsp Dijon mustard

HONEY AND SOY DIP

6 tbsp soy sauce

2 tbsp honey

1 tbsp lime juice

A filling, tasty Chinese soup which makes a meal in itself. You can make it all in one pan, or you could deep-fry the wontons separately.

chilli beef with broth

and goat's cheese dumplings

Heat a large pan over high heat until at smoking point, then add the olive oil. Add the beef, sear on all sides, then remove from the pan with a slotted spoon.

Add all the vegetables to the pan and sauté for 2–3 minutes. Add the thyme, rosemary and vegetable stock. Bring to the boil and cook for about 10 minutes, or until all the vegetables are tender. Return the beef to the broth and stir in the Chinese leaves, beansprouts, coriander and parsley. Simmer for a few minutes, then transfer the soup to a bowl and keep warm. Rinse out the pan.

To make the dumplings, place a ball of goat's cheese in the centre of each wonton wrapper. Brush the edges with beaten egg and gather up to make small bags. Deep-fry at 180°C/350°F for 30 seconds until crisp, then drain on kitchen paper.

Rinse out the pan, then return the soup to the pan to heat through. Serve the soup in a large bowl with the dumplings on top.

you will need

100ml/3½ fl oz olive oil

1kg/2lb sirloin of beef, thinly sliced

3 chillies, deseeded and finely diced

5 shallots, finely sliced

1 courgette, finely diced

2 cloves garlic, finely diced

1 large potato, finely diced

1 large carrot, finely diced

1 tbsp chopped rosemary

1 tbsp thyme leaves

2 heads Chinese leaves, chopped

100g/3½ oz beansprouts

2 tbsp coriander leaves

2 tbsp flat-leaf parsley

Salt and freshly ground black pepper

2 litres/3½ pints Vegetable Stock

(see page 153)

GOAT'S CHEESE DUMPLINGS

8 wonton skins

8 small balls of goat's cheese

1 egg, whisked with a little salt

Vegetable oil, for deep-frying

Serves 6

These tasty 'sandwiches', using deep-fried aubergine slices in place of bread and with a cheese and salad filling, make a very attractive starter, or a quick lunch-time snack.

aubergine, goat's cheese

and pesto sandwich

you will need

3 medium aubergines

Salt

Vegetable oil, for deep frying

2 tbsp balsamic vinegar

90ml/3fl oz virgin olive oil

Freshly ground black pepper

300g/10oz goat's cheese, cut into 1cm/½ in thick slices

2 red peppers, deseeded and cut in strips

9 tsp Basil Pesto (see page 155)

3 tbsp finely shredded rocket leaves

Serves 6

Cut the aubergines into thick slices and sprinkle with salt. Leave on a tray for 1 hour, then dry with kitchen paper to remove the salt.

Heat the oil in a deep-fryer to 180°C/350°F and fry the aubergine slices until golden brown. Remove with a slotted spoon and drain on kitchen paper.

Make a vinaigrette by whisking together the balsamic vinegar, olive oil, salt and pepper.

To make each sandwich, place a slice of aubergine on a plate and top with a slice of goat's cheese. Cover the cheese with some of the pepper strips, then add a teaspoon of pesto. Drizzle with vinaigrette and sprinkle with rocket leaves.

salads etc

The salad is one of the simplest concepts in cooking, the salad bowl being the perfect 'pot' for recipes that are prepared in minutes. Of course, a salad's success lies in its dressing, so I have included a host of oils, vinaigrettes and dressings to make even a simple green salad a delight. This chapter also includes stocks, sauces and accompaniments that are certainly not difficult, but will give your dishes that much-desired professional touch.

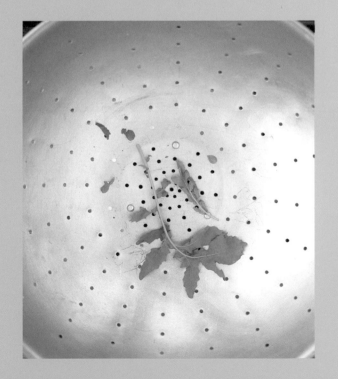

thai salad with nori maki, beans and lime dressing

25g/1oz pickled ginger

4 red salad onions, finely sliced

4 Garlic Confit (see page157

15g/½oz coconut shavings, toasted

2 sprigs coriander

2 sprigs chervil

50g/2oz chives

4 chicken breasts, cooked and diced

1 chilli, deseeded and finely diced

100g/3½oz beansprouts

50g/2oz anchovies, chopped

2 Chinese lettuce leaves, shredded

4 nori maki, shredded finely

1 spring onion, chopped

DRESSING

Zest and juice of 2 limes

4 tbsp olive oil

Salt and freshly ground black pepper

PICKLED CUCUMBER

1 cucumber, peeled, deseeded and diced

4 tsp sesame oil

1 tsp sesame seeds

1 tsp white wine

1 tsp white wine vinegar

½ tsp malt vinegar

2 tbsp honey

Serves 4

To make the pickled cucumber, place the sesame oil, sesame seeds, white wine, vinegars and honey in a small pan and bring to the boil. Add the cucumber and remove from the heat. Leave to cool.

Place all the salad ingredients in a large bowl with 25g/1oz of the pickled cucumber and toss well.

To make the dressing, mix the lime zest and juice with the olive oil and season with salt and pepper. Pour the dressing over the salad and leave to marinate for 1 hour.

fennel salad with red apple, chilli and mustard

4 fennel bulbs

500g/1lb asparagus spears

1 eating apple, cored and diced

75g/3oz chives,chopped

25g/1oz coriander, chopped

1 chilli, deseeded and diced

Juice and zest of 1 lemon

25g/1oz sugar

250g/8oz rocket

100g/3½oz cos lettuce

2 shallots, diced

50ml/2fl oz Balsamic Vinaigrette (see page 154)

1 tbsp grated Parmesan

Salt and freshly ground black pepper

4 tbsp chilli oil

Serves 4

Blanch the fennel and asparagus in a large pan of boiling water, refresh under cold water and drain. Slice the fennel finely.

Mix the apple, chives, coriander, chilli, lemon zest, juice and sugar in a bowl. Add the rocket, cos lettuce, shallots and dressing and toss well. Add the Parmesan and season. Arrange the salad in the centre of a large plate. Lay the asparagus and fennel on top and drizzle with chilli oil.

mixed bean salad with feta and pitta bread

200g/7oz canned flageolet beans

200g/7oz canned blackeye beans

200g/7oz canned butter beans

200g/7oz canned borlotti beans

Salt and freshly ground black pepper

100g/3½oz feta, chopped

20 cherry tomatoes

½ bunch Italian parsley

200g/7oz marinated black olives.

Chopped flat-leaf parsley, to garnish

DRESSING

100g/31/2oz olive oil

2 shallots, finely chopped

2 sprigs thyme, picked

Juice of 2 lemons

Serves 4

Drain all the beans, place in a large bowl and season with salt and pepper. Mix in all the remaining ingredients. Mix the vinaigrette ingredients together, add to the bowl and toss well. Garnish with flat-leaf parsley. Serve with grilled warm pitta bread on the side.

Season and chill. Mix the vegetables and olive oil and leave to marinate for 10 minutes.

green salad

3 heads mache

200g/7oz rocket

Small bunch of tarragon

Small bunch of basil

Small bunch of coriander

Small bunch of chervil

Small bunch of chives, roughly chopped

½ head red oak lettuce

Balsamic Vinaigrette (see page 154) or other dressing

Serves 4

Wash and dry all lettuce and herbs and toss with your favourite dressing. The balsamic vinaigrette goes best with this.

flavoured oils

chilli oil

300ml/½ pint olive oil

2 carrots, finely diced

2 onions, finely diced

3 celery sticks, finely chopped

1 leek, finely chopped

1 clove garlic, chopped

2 sprigs thyme

1 sprig rosemary

500g/1lb red chillies, deseeded and chopped

500g/1lb red peppers, deseeded and chopped

3 tbsp tomato purée

Salt

Heat 3 tablespoons of the olive oil in a heavy-bottomed pan over moderate heat. Add the vegetables, herbs, chillies and peppers, cover and sweat for 5–10 minutes. Add the tomato purée, mix well and cook for 2 minutes. Stir in the remaining olive oil and leave to cook on a low heat until all the vegetables are tender, about 20 minutes. Season with salt, remove from the heat, and leave to cool in the pan. When cool, pass through a fine sieve. Store refrigerated for 3 days .

dill oil

100g/3½ oz dill, finely chopped

200ml/7fl oz olive oil

Juice of 1 lemon

Salt and freshly ground black pepper

Mix all the ingredients together and store for 2-3 days in the refrigerator.

basil oil

100g/3½oz basil leaves

1-2 tbsp water

200ml/7fl oz olive oil

Salt and freshly ground black pepper

1 clove garlic, crushed

Purée the basil with the water in a food processor. Do this quickly, because if you process the basil for too long it will lose its bright colour. Transfer to a bowl and gradually whisk in the oil. Season and add the garlic. Refrigerate for up to 3 days.

tomato oil

200ml/7fl oz olive oil

2 cloves garlic, crushed

2 shallots, chopped

1 celery stick, chopped

¼ fennel bulb, chopped

1 tbsp chopped basil

½ tbsp chopped oregano

2 bay leaves

40ml/1½fl oz tomato purée

Salt and freshly ground black pepper

Heat 1 tablespoon of olive oil in a medium-sized pan and add the garlic, shallots, celery, fennel, basil, oregano and bay leaves. Cover and sweat for 5 minutes over moderate heat until the vegetables are tender, but not coloured. Add the tomato purée and mix well. Continue to cook gently for another 10 minutes, making sure the heat is very low, as the mixture is quite dry and could burn easily. Gradually add the remaining oil, stirring continuously. Season well and cook gently for another 1½-2 hours.

Allow to cool, then pass the mixture through a fine sieve. The oil will have separated from the sediment. For an extra clear oil, strain twice though muslin. Adjust the seasoning if necessary. Store refrigerated for 2-3 days.

beetroot oil

4 beetroot, peeled

Salt and freshly ground black pepper

2 tbsp balsamic vinegar

1 tsp sugar

100ml/3½fl oz olive oil

This is only practical to make when you are cooking beetroot anyway.

Cook the beetroot in boiling salted water until tender, then drain, reserving the liquid. Place the liquid in a pan with the vinegar and sugar and boil until reduced by half. Allow to cool then whisk in the olive oil. Season and refrigerate for up to 2-3 days.

curry oil

2 cloves garlic, roughly chopped

2 shallots, roughly chopped

2 sprigs thyme

3 tbsp curry powder

1 tsp ground cumin

1 tsp fennel seeds, crushed

Salt and freshly ground black pepper

300ml/½ pint olive oil

Preheat the oven to 150°C/300°F/Gas mark 2.

Place all the dry ingredients in a roasting tin. Pour 100ml/3½fl oz of the olive oil over them and roast for 1 hour.

Transfer the ingredients to a medium-sized pan along with the remaining oil and cook over a gentle heat for 2 hours. Remove from the heat and leave to cool overnight. Strain, then store refrigerated for 2-3 days.

stocks

chicken stock

Makes about 1 litre/1¾ pints

2kg/4lb raw chicken bones or carcasses

3 litres/5 pints cold water

1 leek, roughly chopped

1 carrot, roughly chopped

1 onion, unpeeled, roughly chopped

1 sprig rosemary

Salt and freshly ground black pepper

Place the bones in a large pan and add the water. Bring to the boil, skimming off any impurities on the surface. Add the remaining ingredients. Bring to the boil once more, then reduce the heat and simmer gently for at least 4 hours. Skim the stock regularly.

Allow to cool slightly, then remove the bones. Strain through a fine sieve or preferably muslin. Discard the vegetables and bones. Reduce the stock by rapid boiling if it lacks flavour. Otherwise cool and then refrigerate or freeze.

beef or veal stock

Makes about 2 litres/3½ pints

2kg/4lb beef or veal bones

125ml/4fl oz olive oil

Salt and freshly ground black pepper

1 large onion, unpeeled and roughly chopped

2 shallots, unpeeled and roughly chopped

2 large carrots, roughly chopped

2 celery sticks, roughly chopped

4 cloves garlic, chopped

½ bottle red wine

8 litres/14 pints cold water

1 bay leaf

1 sprig thyme

Preheat the oven to 200°C/400°F/Gas mark 6. Place the bones in a large roasting tin. Brush with 200ml/7fl oz of the olive oil and season well. Roast in the oven for up to 2 hours until very well browned.

Heat the remaining olive oil in a very large pan and sauté the onion, shallots, carrots, celery and garlic until well browned. Add the red wine and simmer until reduced by half. Add the water, mix well, and add the bones. Bring to the boil and simmer uncovered for at least 4 hours, skimming off any fat or impurities that rise to the surface. Add more water if necessary, as the bones must be kept covered.

Remove the bones, strain the stock through a colander and then through muslin or a fine sieve. Transfer to a clean pan and boil until reduced by at least half. Allow to cool and reheat or freeze as required.

lamb stock

Makes 500ml/16fl oz

2 tbsp olive oil

1kg/2lb lamb bones

10 shallots, roughly chopped

Salt and freshly ground black pepper

2 cloves garlic, crushed

1 tbsp grated fresh horseradish

1 tbsp tomato purée

½ teaspoon chopped tarragon

2 sprigs rosemary

1.5 litres/2½ pints Chicken Stock (see left)

or water

Preheat the oven to 200°C/400°F/Gas mark 6. Pour 1 tablespoon of olive oil into a large roasting tin. Add the bones and roast in the oven until well browned, about 40 minutes. Turn the bones occasionally to ensure an even colour.

Meanwhile, heat the remaining olive oil in a large pan and sauté the shallots. Season with a little salt and pepper. When the shallots have browned evenly, add the garlic, horseradish and tomato purée. Cook for a further 5 minutes and then add the herbs, stock or water. Bring to the boil, then reduce the heat and simmer for 3 hours. Skim the stock regularly to remove any fat or impurities that rise to the surface.

When the stock is ready, remove the bones and pass the stock through a fine sieve or muslin 3 times. Transfer to a clean pan and boil until reduced to about half. Allow to cool, then refrigerate or freeze.

vegetable stock

Makes 500ml/16fl oz

50g/2oz butter

2 courgettes, roughly chopped

2 leeks, roughly chopped

2 carrots, roughly chopped

2 celery sticks, roughly chopped

5 cloves garlic, crushed

1 fennel bulb, roughly chopped

1 onion, roughly chopped

1.5 litres/21/2 pints water

1 tbsp chopped basil

1 tbsp chopped tarragon

Salt and freshly ground black pepper

Place all the ingredients except the herbs and water in a large pan and cook for 15 minutes over a gentle heat. Add the water, which should cover the vegetables, and cook for a further 15 minutes. Remove from the heat and add the herbs. Leave to stand for 5 minutes, then strain. Return the stock to the pan and boil until reduced by about half. Season lightly. Allow to cool, then refrigerate or freeze.

vinaigrettes

lemongrass vinaigrette

1 stalk lemongrass

150ml/¼ pint olive oil

60ml/2fl oz tarragon vinegar

1 tsp sugar

Salt and freshly ground black pepper

Serves 4

Bruise the lemongrass using a rolling pin or the bottom of a pan. Place the olive oil in a small pan with the lemongrass and heat through for 1 minute, then leave to infuse for 15 minutes. Mix together the tarragon vinegar, sugar, salt and pepper. Remove the lemon grass from the olive oil and discard. Gradually whisk the olive oil into the tarragon vinegar. Refrigerate until ready to use.

truffle vinaigrette

125ml/4fl oz olive oil

30ml/1fl oz balsamic vinegar

1 tsp sugar

1 tbsp truffle trimmings

1 tsp truffle oil

1 tomato, skinned, deseeded and finely diced

1 small bunch chives, finely chopped

Salt and freshly ground black pepper

Serves 4

Whisk the first 5 ingredients together in a bowl. Leave to stand for 2-3 hours to allow the flavours to develop. Just before serving, mix in the tomato and chives. Season and serve immediately.

carrot and ginger vinaigrette

2 tbsp olive oil

2 carrots, chopped

2 shallots, chopped

2.5cm/1in root ginger, peeled and finely chopped

Knob of butter

1 clove garlic, crushed

Pinch of saffron

1 sprig thyme

1 sprig rosemary

200ml/7fl oz Chicken Stock

(see page 153)

60ml/2fl oz double cream

Salt and freshly ground black pepper

Heat the olive oil in a pan over moderate heat. Add the carrots and shallots and sweat for 10 minutes. Add the ginger and butter. Cook gently, adding the garlic, saffron and herbs. Season.

Add the stock, allow to heat up then simmer for 5–10 minutes. Stir in the cream and allow to cool. Blend in a food processor, then pass through a sieve into a clean pan. Reduce over moderate heat until thick and creamy. Add seasoning. Reheat if necessary.

ginger and basil vinaigrette

125ml/4fl oz olive oil

30ml/1fl oz balsamic vinegar

1 shallot, roughly chopped

1 clove garlic, crushed

1 tbsp basil leaves

2.5cm/1in root ginger, peeled and finely chopped

1 tsp warm water

1 egg yolk (optional)

Salt and freshly ground black pepper

Serves 4

Place all the ingredients in a blender or food processor and blend until smooth. Refrigerate until ready to use. Use within 24 hours.

champagne vinaigrette

125ml/4fl oz olive oil

2 tbsp good quality champagne vinegar

½ shallot, roughly chopped

½ tsp sugar

Salt and freshly ground black pepper

To make the vinaigrette, place all the ingredients in a blender and process until smooth. Refrigerate until ready to use. Use within 3-4 days.

balsamic vinaigrette

125ml/4fl oz olive oil

30ml/1fl oz good quality balsamic vinegar

½ shallot, roughly chopped

½ teaspoon sugar

Salt and freshly ground black pepper

Place all the ingredients in a blender or food processor and blend until smooth. Refrigerate until ready to use. Use within 3-4 days.

walnut vinaigrette

1 tsp Dijon mustard

30ml/1fl oz white wine vinegar

Salt and freshly ground black pepper

60ml/2fl oz walnut oil

60ml/2fl oz groundnut oil

Whisk the mustard, vinegar, salt and pepper together then gradually whisk in the oils. Refrigerate until ready to use.

sauces and accompaniments

basil pesto

25g/1oz basil leaves

25g/1oz grated Parmesan

3 cloves garlic, chopped

15g/½oz roasted pine nuts

2 tbsp olive oil

Salt and freshly ground black pepper

Combine all dry ingredients in a food processor and slowly add the olive oil. Season well with salt and pepper. Store in a glass jar in the fridge for up to 1 week .

chilli jam

100ml/3½fl oz white vinegar

75g/3oz sugar

100ml/3½fl oz white wine

150g/5oz red chillies, deseeded and roughly chopped

25g/1oz butter

1 sprig thyme

Salt and freshly ground black pepper

Heat the vinegar and sugar in a pan until it has a syrup-like consistency. Bring to the boil and add the white wine. Bring back to the boil and add the chillies. Cook over high heat for 20 minutes, then add the butter and thyme. Blend in a food processor, season and allow to cool.

oven-dried tomatoes

8 plum tomatoes, halved

Rock salt

2 sprigs thyme

3 cloves garlic, sliced

3 tbsp olive oil

Place the tomatoes in a roasting tin and sprinkle with the rock salt, thyme, garlic and olive oil. Place them in the oven at the lowest possible setting and leave to dry out overnight.

onion and coriander marmalade

2 tbsp olive oil

8 red onions, finely sliced

75g/3oz butter

Salt and freshly ground black pepper

100g/3½oz sugar

1 sprig thyme

1 tbsp red wine vinegar

100ml/3½fl ozgrenadine

100ml/3½fl oz red wine

50ml/2fl oz Chicken Stock (see page 153)

50g/2oz coriander, roughly chopped

Heat the olive oil in a large pan over moderate heat and add the onions. Sauté for 2-3 minutes, then add the butter, salt, pepper, sugar, thyme and vinegar. Cook for another 2-3 minutes until the butter has melted and the sugar has dissolved, then increase the heat and allow to caramelise slightly. Add the grenadine, red wine and stock. Continue to cook over a high heat until the liquid had reduced and the onions have a jam-like consistency. Add the coriander, adjust the seasoning and allow to cool.

sun-dried tomato tapenade

250g/8oz sun-dried tomatoes in oil, drained

40g/2½oz black olives, stoned

1 small bunch chives, roughly chopped

1 tbsp chopped parsley

1 tbsp chopped coriander

4 cloves garlic, roughly chopped

1 tbsp anchovy paste

50ml/2fl oz olive oil

Salt and freshly ground black pepper

Blend all the ingredients together in a food processor until the texture is very fine. Push through a fine sieve, using the back of a wooden spoon. Adjust the seasoning if necessary and serve.
To store, spoon into a jar, top up with olive oil and keep sealed.

garlic cream

4 cloves garlic, very finely crushed

200ml /7fl oz double cream

100ml/3½fl oz Chicken Stock (see page 153)

1 sprig rosemary

1 sprig thyme

Place all ingredients together in a small pan and boil rapidly until reduced by a quarter. Strain and reheat if necessary.

red pepper coulis

100/3½oz butter

4 red peppers, deseeded and diced

4 shallots, diced

1 leek, white part only, diced

1 celery stick, diced

2 cloves garlic, crushed

1 sprig thyme

1 bay leaf

Salt and freshly ground black pepper

Sugar 500ml/16fl oz tomato juice

Melt the butter in a pan over moderate heat and add the vegetables, garlic and herbs. Cook gently until tender. Season and add sugar to taste. Add the tomato juice and simmer until the peppers are tender. Blend in a processor then push through a fine sieve. Season, and add water if necessary to give a pouring consistency.

watercress purée

25g/1oz butter

100g/3½oz watercress

1 litre/1¾ pints double cream

Salt and freshly ground black pepper

Melt the butter in a pan over moderate heat and sauté the watercress until tender. Add enough of the cream to cover. Blend until smooth in a food processor, then push through a fine sieve and return to a clean pan. Add more cream, season and reduce slightly.

parmesan cream

4 egg yolks

600ml/1 pint olive oil

200ml/7fl oz groundnut oil

200g/7oz grated Parmesan

3 shallots, finely diced

2 cloves garlic, crushed

1 sprig thyme, leaves picked

2 tbsp champagne vinegar

Salt and freshly ground black pepper

In a food processor, blend the egg yolks and oil until it is the consistency of mayonnaise. Add the Parmesan, shallots, garlic and thyme. Blend again until the texture is smooth. Add the vinegar, salt and pepper.

langoustine sauce

500/1lb langoustine shells

1 carrot, chopped

1 Spanish onion, chopped

4 shallots, chopped

1 head garlic

½ fennel bulb, chopped

1 small red chilli, deseeded

6 vine tomatoes

2 tbsp Tomato Fondue (see page 157)

1/2 tbsp chopped parsley

100ml/3½fl oz dry martini

100ml/3½fl oz brandy

100ml/3½fl oz white wine

200ml/7fl oz fish stock

400ml/14fl oz double cream

Place the langoustine shells in a wide pan and roast over a high heat for about 5 minutes. Add the carrot, onion, shallots, garlic, fennel, chilli, tomatoes and tomato fondue and allow to caramelise for about 5 minutes. Add the martini and brandy and heat for 2-3 minutes to drive off the alcohol. Add the white wine and fish stock. Simmer gently for about 2 hours on a low heat. Pass through a fine sieve, return to a clean pan and heat until reduced to half a litre. Add the cream and simmer gently for about 5 minutes.

tomato sauce

Olive oil

8 plum tomatoes

2 cloves garlic, crushed

4 shallots, diced

Sprig of thyme

Sprig of rosemary

1 red pepper, deseeded and diced

1 red chilli, deseeded and diced

2 tbsp Tomato Fondue (see page 157)

½ vanilla pod

Salt and freshly ground black pepper

600ml/1 pint Chicken Stock (see page 153)

Heat the olive oil in a medium-sized pan over moderate heat. Slowly add the tomatoes, garlic,

shallots, thyme, rosemary, pepper, chilli, tomato fondue, and vanilla pod. Stir gently, season and add the chicken stock. Simmer gently for 20 minutes and pass through a fine sieve.

mushroom sauce

250g/8oz button mushrooms

2 cloves garlic, diced

1 sprig thyme

8 shallots, diced

1 carrot, finely diced

1 leek (white part only), diced

Lemon zest

Orange zest

1 vanilla pod

200g/7oz sugar

1 red pepper, deseeded and diced

500ml/16fl oz balsamic vinegar

300ml/½ pint Chicken Stock

(see page 153)

Place all ingredients in a large casserole over moderate heat. Simmer until reduced by half. Pass the sauce through a fine sieve.

pesto couscous

25g/1oz butter

300g/10oz couscous

300ml/½ pint Chicken or Vegetable Stock (see page 153)

4 tbsp Basil Pesto (see page 155)

Juice of 2 lemons

Melt the butter in a medium-sized-pan over gentle heat. Add the couscous and cook for 1 minute, stirring. Heat the stock to boiling point and stir into the couscous. Stir in the pesto and lemon juice.

goat's cheese cream

400g/14oz soft goat's cheese

2 tomatoes, roughly chopped

3 tbsp chopped basil

Freshly ground black pepper

1-2 tbsp double cream

Mix all the ingredients together to make a smooth paste. Add more cream if you want to thin out the consistency. Use on canapés.

pepper stew

4 shallots, finely diced

2 cloves garlic, crushed and finely diced

1 red onion, finely diced

1 green pepper, deseeded and finely diced

1 yellow pepper, deseeded and finely diced

1 red pepper, deseeded and finely diced

1 sprig thyme, leaves picked

2 tbsp Tomato Fondue (see right)

Sauté the shallots, garlic and red onion in a hot frying pan for 1 minute. Add the peppers and thyme and cook for 5–6 minutes. Allow to cool and stir in the tomato fondue.

garlic confit

Using the duck or goose fat will give a better flavour.

16 cloves garlic, unpeeled

Vegetable oil, duck fat or goose fat

1 bay leaf

1 sprig rosemary

1 sprig thyme

4 black peppercorns

Bring a small pan of water to the boil and blanch the garlic for 1 minute. Remove with a slotted spoon, refresh under cold running water, then return to the pan. Repeat the blanching and

refreshing twice more.

Meanwhile, heat the oil or fat in a small pan to about 90°C/195°F. Add the garlic and remaining ingredients and cook at 80°C/175°F for about 10 minutes. The garlic should be tender, but not too coloured. Drain on kitchen paper and serve immediately, or allow to cool in the fat and keep in the fridge for up to 1 week.

tomato fondue

1 tablespoon olive oil

4 shallots, finely chopped

2 cloves garlic, crushed

8 plum tomatoes, skinned, deseeded and chopped

1 sprig thyme

1 sprig rosemary

1 tablespoon tomato purée

Salt and freshly ground black pepper

Heat the oil in a pan over a moderate heat and sweat the shallots and garlic until soft but not coloured. Add the tomatoes, herbs and tomato purée. Simmer gently until the liquid has all evaporated and the mixture is quite dry. Season well and allow to cool. Refrigerate until ready to use.

beef jus

750ml/1¼ pints Beef Stock (see page 153)

75g/3oz butter

2 tbsp olive oil

Bring the beef stock to the boil in a large pan, then simmer until reduced by one-third. Whisk in the butter and olive oil and adjust the seasoning.

index

acknowledgements

The publisher would like to thank the following for their kind assistance in lending props for photoshoots: Nicole Farhi (0171 494 9051), Mint (0171 224 4406), The Conran Shop (0171 589 7401) and Divertimenti (0171 581 8065).